Tripping and Slipping Litigation

CW00819890

Tripping and Slipping Litigation

by
Denis Carey BA LLM
Solicitor and Attorney at Law

EMIS Professional Publishing Ltd

© Denis Carey 2003

Published by
EMIS Professional Publishing Ltd
31–33 Stonehills House
Howardsgate
Welwyn Garden City
AL8 6PU

ISBN 1 85811 285 0

Typeset by Jane Conway
Cover by Jane Conway

Printed by Intypelibra

Contents

Preface

In the first edition I attempted to write a book which presented in a clear and accessible manner the key information associated with this area of personal injury practice. My efforts seemed to meet with some success; reviews (and sales) have been heartening. In this second edition, I have carried on the approach I originally adopted. I have continued to strive for simplicity of presentation, and I hope I have not had to sacrifice too much in the way of detail to achieve my aim.

I have left the layout of the text little changed. I have given some more attention to a number of areas – in particular, to the section 58 defence, to winter cases (after the House of Lords decision in *Goodes*), to expanding the precedents in the Appendix and to ensuring that they comply with the CPR.

There are other works which deal with this topic, either in its entirety or concentrating on particular aspects, in much greater depth. This text looks at the subject from the perspective of the busy practitioner acting for the claimant. With a fixed-costs regime looming, it aims to be a useful and concise summary of the important areas of law which arise in this type of case. Where a fuller treatment is required the reader is directed to suitable sources.

As ever, I am indebted to those of my colleagues who read and commented upon drafts of the text, and am obliged for the improvements they suggested.

I am in particular obliged to Paul Davis, Barrister and former partner in Russell Jones Walker's Leeds office who read the sections of the manuscript which relate to occupiers liability. His comments and suggestions have been invaluable. Any errors or omissions are, of course, mine.

Finally I am as usual grateful for the forbearance of Andrew Griffin of EMIS Publishers in awaiting a very much overdue piece of work without complaint.

The reader might note that for consistency I have followed the convention of using "claimant" in the place of "plaintiff" throughout, even when referring to a party in a pre-CPR case, except when quoting directly from a judgment. I have endeavoured to ensure that the law stated is as of February 2003.

Denis Carey
February 2003

Acknowledgements

Statutory extracts and other Crown Copyright material reproduced with kind permission of HMSO.

Disclaimer

Table of Cases

Table of Statutes

Table of Statutory Instruments

SECTION 1
General Overview

CHAPTER 1

Introduction

Introduction

Background

"Personal injury claims are here to stay, and they are growing rapidly. It is up to the [claimant] and the defendant sides to establish rules of engagement in this volatile and unpredictable market."[1]

So said Datamonitor, a leading business information company specialising in industry analysis, in June 2001. Their next report, in 2002, noted:

- approx 1.8 million accidents a year in the UK could result in a personal injury claim due to the fact that they can be partly, or wholly, attributed to another party;

- in the year 2001 to 2002 there were a total of 614,000 personal injury claims made to insurers.

According to Datamonitor:

- 78 per cent of people feel it is morally and socially acceptable to pursue a personal injury claim;

- 72 per cent of people would consider making a claim if they were injured as a result of someone else's fault.

- the frequency of personal injury claims is increasing due to:
  i. increased exposure by the media;
  ii. advertising campaigns by solicitors and others;
  iii. the involvement of accident intermediaries;
  iv. governmental reforms to the legislative process.

While no figures are available which separate out the number of trips and slips from the above figures, it is obvious to any practitioner that this type of claim makes up a substantial segment of the personal injury

---

1 *UK Personal Injury Litigation 2001; Surviving and Thriving in the Compensation Culture*, Datamonitor report 6 June 2001.

claim sector. That sector continues to grow, and therefore a thorough grasp of this topic becomes of ever greater importance to the claimant PI lawyer.

General Overview

Although tripping and slipping cases are among the most common of personal injury matters, they are also potentially the most difficult, particularly in the area of establishing liability. Because of this many practitioner texts become overwritten and textually dense, despite their authors' best endeavours. This practice text aims to provide an accessible guide to the law relating to the three main locii of trips and slips – **highways, premises and workplaces** – and seeks to present in clear language and in an uncomplicated format the relevant case law and legislation.

The text is intended to guide the specialist and non-specialist personal injury lawyer alike. For more detailed treatment of particular issues litigators' attention is drawn to the works referenced in the text or set out in the bibliography. The reader won't find a discussion of the finer or more esoteric points of law – so attractive to the academic lawyer or to counsel – here. This text deals with the realities of tripping & slipping litigation in practice, concentrating on those problems encountered on a day-by-day basis by the practitioner.

Slips and Trips

Slips and trips are a significant cause of personal injuries generally, and the average case falls in the **medium to severe** loss and damage range.

Slipping, tripping and falling, collectively, constitute the single most common cause of injuries at work,[2] for example. There are very few people who have not at some time slipped or tripped. What we are concerned here is obtaining a remedy for those slips and trips which result in injury, and which are actionable.

The number of accidents which fall into our class is vast.

---

2 See *Slips, Trips and Falls at Work* Health and Safety Monitor. Jul. 1996, vol. 19, no. 7, 5–7.

Definitions

A **trip** occurs when a lower limb in forward motion is unexpectedly impeded. A **slip** occurs when a foot which is about to make contact with a floor surface slides backwards, forwards or sideways usually as a result of surface glossing or contamination.

Deciding whether a surface is slippery is usually more difficult than identifying tripping situations, which typically turn on easily measured protrusions, obstructions or pits. Slipping, or rather resistance to slipping, is measured by what is termed the "coefficient of friction", where zero indicates perfect sliding and one indicates a frictional force equal to that keeping resting surfaces together.

Avoidance of Slips and Trips

Of course every slip and trip claimant has a duty not to contribute to the accident. That is dealt with below in the section on contributory negligence. What we look at here is a brief overview of avoidance techniques, mainly in the slipping context, which it is argued should be practised by reasonably **careful individuals responsible for any surfaces** over which others pass on foot or otherwise. The slip and trip practitioner will of course **look for the absence** of these measures. (See Appendix 4 for a **checklist** of measures suggested by HSE for a particular industry[3] which can be adapted to suit many other circumstances).

Points to be addressed

Whether the accident took place on a highway, premises or workplace, check whether the following points were taken into consideration by the potential defendant:

- surfacing materials characteristics
- volume of traffic
- nature of traffic
- possibility of substance contamination

---

3   Health and Safety Executive *Slips and Trips – Guidance for the Food Processing Industry* (HMSO) 1996.

- temperature range
- inspection arrangements
- cleaning and/or clearing arrangements
- maintenance arrangements

Care, cleaning, litter and hazard removal, general maintenance – these are all areas of enquiry. The practitioner may have to know or find out about some quite esoteric matters – interaction between different types of flooring, long term ancillary damage,[4] hazards requiring special care and so forth.

The next section deals briefly with these and other matters in the context of **case preparation.**

---

4 For example, anti-slip treatments are often acid based and long term use may transform the hazard into a tripping situation. Then again, some anti-slip treatments if used on the wrong type of flooring actually increase the hazard.

CHAPTER 2

Case Preparation

Case Preparation

Initial Points

This is not a general personal injury text, and it is assumed that the practitioner using it will have some familiarity with basic good practice and efficient case handling. However, there are some aspects of case preparation which will pay dividends if followed carefully in trip and slip cases in particular. A little time is taken here, therefore, to look at certain steps which, if taken at the outset, will promote successful case resolution.

Since the first edition of this text so-called "accident intermediaries" have entered the litigation field. These firms advertise for individuals who have suffered accidental injuries and promise to obtain compensation on their behalf. We are not concerned here with whether such businesses are beneficial to their clients or to society. What we are concerned with is the fact that they have raised general awareness of the possibility of obtaining compensation for injury suffered. Unfortunately, a small number of individuals have seen an opportunity of making claims for fictitious accidents, or of exaggerating the symptoms of minor accidental trauma actually suffered. Fictitious or exaggerated claims have always been encountered in personal injury litigation but there is a perception that the proportion of them has increased in recent times. Accordingly, the trip & slip litigation professional has a duty not to be over-credulous. Properly carried out, in-depth early investigation will in most cases show up the dubious cases. Watch for:

- uncertainty about the date of the accident

- failure to report the alleged accident to an authority

- lack of an entry in an accident book

- inconsistencies between GP records and the claimant's account

- inconsistencies between hospital records and the claimant's account and where you have doubts do not hestitate to question the claimant in greater detail.

If you do not have confidence in the claimant's account now is the time to regretfully decline to act in the matter, perhaps suggesting that further advice be sought elsewhere and, always, giving a written limitation warning.

First Interview

This is where it is established whether or not the claimant has a valid slip and trip case. Extra time spent here will will pay for itself later – information gained will determine the conduct and outcome of the action.

In slip and trip cases it is important to explain to the claimant exactly what needs to be established. It is vital that any popular misconceptions held by the injured party are dispelled. Many victims of slipping or tripping accidents are under the impression that they are entitled to compensation merely because they have suffered injury.

In some cases the claimant will have walked in "off the street". In that case the questionnaire referred to below will be invaluable. However, in most cases an appointment will have been arranged for the initial interview. In that situation it is a good idea to have asked the claimant to bring a written account of how the slip or trip occurred. A photo or sketch should be asked for in all cases.

Evidence Gathering

A slip and trip litigator will usually use the details from the initial interview/the proofing process to put together the claimant's witness statement. Preparing the witness statement is a vital part of the litigation process.

Remember:

- the witness statement is a reduction of the information extracted from the claimant during the proofing process;

- the claim will be pleaded from the witness statement;

- it forms the bedrock upon with the structure of the slip and trip case will be built.

Claimant's Witness Statement

The Civil Procedure Rules

The overriding principle of fairness, the concept of proportionality, the necessity of dealing with matters swiftly and cost-effectively all mean that tripping and slipping litigation must be handled with great efficiency.

The proof of evidence process is the method by which the fullest possible detail is extracted from a claimant in trip and slip matters.

- The Proof is not a Witness Statement. A Witness Statement contains only matters a claimant can prove; a Proof can contain assertions, whether or not they can be substantiated.

- The Witness Statement will be drafted from the contents of the Proof.

- A Proof does not have to be disclosed to the other side, unlike a Witness Statement.

- Remember who will be using the Proof – it is intended to help you and Counsel.

- Proofs are usually taken at the first interview, either directly or from notes.

Remembering the use to which the Proof will be put, a degree of meticulousness in its preparation will be well rewarded. It should be chronological, methodical and comprehensive.

After the actual injury/ies, which the medical report will deal with, it is the effect on the claimant's day to day activities such as work, social life, relationships and so for the which will determine the level of damages. It is crucial to address these issues thoroughly.

Evidence Questionnaire

It is good practice in most (possibly all) slip and trip cases to use a questionnaire.[5] The following headings can be used by a practitioner to construct one according to personal preferences. Most of the following information will be sought in all cases, with adaptations for individual circumstances.

Personal Details

- the claimant's name, address, date of birth

- the claimant's home and work phone numbers

- the claimant's personal circumstances – marital status, whether living alone or with a partner and whether there are any children

- full details should be taken of spouse/partner/children as the claimant's obligations to these may well affect quantum

- full details of the next friend if applicable

- educational history and employment history (whether or not a workplace related claim)

- current employment details

The trip or slip

The accident/incident details are sought next:

- the date, time and place
- ask the client for his or her own account of what happened
- a sketch should be made by the client
- photographs should be arranged (see below)
- witness details – important

---

5   One such questionnaire is published by EMIS Professional Publishing as part of its MLQ System.

Accidents at work

If it is a workplace accident some additional questions must be asked:

- the claimant's exact job description/status
- was someone other than the claimant also involved?
- what training had been given to the claimant?
- the supervision arrangements must be determined
- were there were earlier similar accidents?
- had any complaints were made to the employer?
- was there an accident report?
- to whom was it made?
- was it recorded in an accident book?
- was the Health and Safety Executive involved?

Case investigation

Witnesses

In many slip and trip cases the litigator will urgently need to make enquiries of any witnesses to the accident.

Most litigators will have a stock precedent letter to witnesses which can be adapted as required. In slip and trip cases the letter should contain the following:

- name and address of client
- date, time and place of slip/trip
- statement that it is believed that the addressee witnessed the slip/trip
- request for brief statement of what occurred
- specific request for evaluation of blame
- if appropriate, request for sketch map
- stamped addressed envelope
- expression of appreciation for assistance

Where the accident took place at work the letter should in addition ask whether the witness is aware of any similar accidents having taken place previously.

Accident and Emergency Treatment

Was the claimant taken to A & E by ambulance? If so, the crew may have relevant evidence. The ambulance service may provide a report if informed of the date and time of the accident. In the alternative, the service may identify the individual crew members, who can be asked individually.

A report should be requested from the medical records section of any hospital to which the claimant attended, or was taken to, for treatment.

Health and Safety Executive

Only very serious accidents at work are investigated by this body and in most slip and trip cases there will be no HSE involvement. However, if a report exists it is absolutely vital that a copy is obtained.

In any event, it is good practice to write to the HSE in any fairly serious work-related slip and trip, asking whether a report was prepared and requesting a copy of same if there is one.

Disclosure

The claimant should provide, with the letter of claim if possible, a list of the documents he considers to be relevant and believed to be in the possession of the defendant.

Disclosure is the term for what was previously termed discovery. The CPR seeks to make the process simpler than before, and a party is only required to make **standard disclosure** unless otherwise ordered. The Protocol says that the aim of the early disclosure of documents by the defendant is not to encourage "fishing expeditions" by the claimant, but to promote an early exchange of relevant information to help in clarifying or resolving issues in dispute. In practice, this means a party is required to disclose:

- The documents on which he relies;
- The documents which could adversely affect his case;
- The documents which could adversely affect another party's case;
- The documents which could support another party's case;
- Any documents required further to a practice direction.

Specific disclosure applies where a party wishes the other side to produce a particular document. In trips and slips this will sometimes arise in accidents at work, where the claimant will know of a relevant document in the defendant's possession. An application for specific disclosure must be supported by evidence, and will be granted if necessary to fairly dispose of the claim or to save costs (any document mentioned in another party's statement of case, witness statements, experts' reports or affidavits may be inspected as of right).

The documents disclosed as a matter of practice in highway tripping and slipping cases will include:

- Highway inspection records
- Highway authority maintenance records
- Complaints records
- Accident records

The Local Government (Access to Information) Act 1985 provides that the minutes of council meetings must be open to the public for inspection at the council's offices for a period of six years. Therefore, the record of any relevant highway authority meetings at which highway maintenance or inspection policy was discussed will be easily obtainable.

Specialist Inspection

In the case of some slip and trips (particularly workplace related) it will be necessary to obtain specialist advice, opinions and reports. Slips and trips are notorious for the rapidity with which the locus alters. Immediate inspection and evidence gathering is vital.

In certain circumstances an expert's report will be required before the Particulars or Statement of Claim can be prepared. For example, in a slip/trip at work the expert may need to inspect the premises, observe the process and so forth. A request that facilities to inspect be made available should be made immediately. If a refusal ensues then an application may be made to the court seeking an order that the defendant allows inspection.

Destruction of Evidence

This is by no means unknown in slip and trip cases. If it appears that a defendant is destroying or removing evidence then the court has power to make an order for its preservation.

In tripping cases it is surprising how quickly the offending hole or protrusion is repaired or removed. The more cynical practitioner may believe this is not merely to avoid another accident happening. Anecdotal evidence leads one to the conclusion, alas, that it is not unknown for even local authorities to resort to such practices. There is a responsibility on the litigator to ensure that photographs are taken as soon as possible. Measurements should be accurately made and carefully recorded. The measuring device (e.g. engineer's ruler) should be photographed *in situ*. It cannot be stressed enough that obtaining the evidence quickly is vital in these cases.

It is worth seeking an undertaking from the other side to preserve evidence even in cases where the defendant appears to be co-operative, as attitudes may subsequently change.

SECTION 2
Highways

Trip and Slip – Types of Cases

For ease of reference this text divides slips and trips into three broad categories, based on where they occur –

- trips and slips on **highways**
- trips and slips on **premises**
- trips and slips at **work**

and we now move on to examine the first of these.

CHAPTER 3

Highways – Classification and Creation

Highways – Classification and Creation

Classification of Highways

Repair is the important factor for the trip & slip litigator. For the purposes of slip and trip litigation, from a practical perspective, we say a highway is either

- one which is repairable by a **public authority**

- one which is repairable **privately**

- one for which **no authority or individual** is responsible

The first of these is by far and away the most important, and we concentrate upon it in this text. With privately repairable highways, or where nobody is responsible for repair, consider general tort principles – negligence, nuisance – or statutory duty under the Occupiers' Liability Acts.[6]

However, the above three-part division in itself assumes an understanding of what defines a highway in the first instance, which is where we encounter some difficulty, as we now see.

What is a Highway?

For the definitive treatment of what constitutes a highway, to a depth of detail much greater than we have need of here, but yet eminently readable, you are directed to Volume 20 (1999 Reissue) *Highways, Streets and Bridges* of *Halsbury's Statutes of England and Wales*[7] and to Sauvain's

---

6 For a short treatment on this subject, see Foster, C *Tripping and Slipping Cases: A Practitioner's Guide* (Sweet & Maxwell) 3rd ed. 2002.
7 Fourth Edition, Butterworths, ISBN 0–406–98987–7.

Highway Law, 2nd Edition[8]. For a clear and very straightforward treatment see also Orlik's *An Introduction to Highway Law.*[9]

At common law it has been held[10] that a "highway" is a way over which:

- every member of the general public
- has right of passage
- without let or hindrance

There are at least six essential requirements which must be present before a way is a highway. Firstly, it must in fact be a "way", that is a defined route from one place to another. Then:

- Use must be public – it must be open to all persons (but may be limited to a class or classes of traffic)

- Use must be free – except for statutory tolls there must be no money payment needed for use

- Use must be at will – at any time of the day or night and for as long as one wishes without needing anyone's permission and regardless of any landowner's objections

- Use must include repassage – one must be able to pass and re-pass

- Use must be unobstructed – no barriers, and must be over open land

The term "highway" applies not only to streets and roads, but also to walkways, footpaths, cycle tracks, public paths and bridleways.

Section 130 of the Highways Act 1980 provides that a highway authority has a duty to protect this general right to the use and enjoyment of a highway.

---

8   Sauvain, S.J. *Highway Law Second Edition*, Sweet & Maxwell 1997 ISBN 0–421–562307.
9   Orlik, M *An Introduction to Highway Law*, Shaw & Sons Limited 1996.
10 *Ex parte Lewis* (1888) 21 QBD 191.

Statutory Definition of a Highway

Unfortunately, there is no statutory definition which is particularly useful. Section 328 (1) of the Highways Act 1980 provides:

> [1] In this Act, except where the context otherwise requires, 'highway' means the whole or part of a highway other than a ferry or waterway.
>
> [2] Where a highway passes over a bridge or through a tunnel, that bridge or tunnel is to be taken for the purposes of this Act to be a part of the highway.
>
> [3] In this Act, "highway maintainable at the public expense" and any other expression defined by reference to a highway is to be construed in accordance with the foregoing provisions of this section

In other words, "highway" means "highway", which is not a great deal of assistance to us.

Slip and trip claimants will use words such as **"road"** and **"street"**. In practice, you will find both of these will usually turn out to be highways; see below however in relation to the definition of "street" in the New Roads and Street Works Act 1991.

Section 192 of the Road Traffic Act 1988 defines "road" as "any highway and any other road to which the public has access".[11] In *Clarke* v *Kato*[12] the Court of Appeal held that unrestricted pedestrian user, with or without use by wheeled traffic, was sufficient to establish a road within the meaning of that section.

In so far as "streets" are concerned see the section on statutory undertakers and the New Roads and Street Works Act 1991 below.

It does help somewhat, when trying to grasp what constitutes a highway, to further divide the three above classifications into two broad sub-categories:

- carriageway highways
- non-carriageway highways

---

11 See *Cutter* v *Eagle Star Insurance Co. Ltd* (1996) *The Independent* 3 December (CA).
12 *Clarke* v *Kato* (1966) *The Times* 11 December (CA).

Carriageway Highways

In order for a way to be a highway there must be at the very least a right of way by foot. But what about non-pedestrian traffic? Carriageway highways are defined in the Highways Act 1980, section 329(1) as a way:

> "...constituting or comprised in a highway, being a way (other than a cycle track) over which the public has a right of way for the passage of vehicles."

Most carriageways are in fact "all purpose" ways – that is, the public has a right to use them in vehicles, on foot and even on horseback. Note however that section 16 of the Highways Act 1980 authorises a Highway Authority to construct "special roads" for the use of a specified class or classes of traffic. This is the section that the Secretary of State for Transport, being the Highway Authority for trunk roads, uses when making a Scheme authorising the building of a motorway. A motorway is a highway[13] but one which cannot be used by those on foot or on horseback, among other restrictions.

Carriageway Footways

A path for pedestrians by the side of a carriageway highway is a footway, and forms part of it, with pedestrians having the right to use the entirety (i.e. the part other than the footway also). Note that there is a conflict as to whether the carriageway of a road must be as safe for those on foot as the pedestrian path.[14]

---

13 Section 329 of the Highways Act 1980.
14 See the different decisions in *Bird v Tower Hamlets London Borough Council* (1969) 67 LGR 682 (where a depression in a carriageway which would not have affected wheeled traffic made the authority liable to a pedestrian) and *Ford v Liverpool Corporation* (1972) 117 SJ 167 (no liability for metal protrusion in carriageway of over one inch, which would have attracted liability on a footway).

Non-carriageway Highways

Non-carriageway highways are also highways for slip and trip purposes. The main types consist of:

- **cycle tracks** – section 329[1] of the Highways Act 1980 provides these are ways constituting or comprised in a highway over which there is a public right of way on pedal cycles, with or without a right of way on foot, and over which there is no other right of way.

- **walkways** – these are always attached to a building. An example is the means of ingress and egress to and from a multi-storey car park attached to and forming part of a shopping complex. Walkways can be over, under or through a building. They must be created by agreement – see section 35 of the Highways Act 1980. They can cause difficulties in slip and trip scenarios; liability for their maintenance must be individually ascertained in each case. The more pedantic lawyer might ask whether walkways are in fact highways at all, as many are locked shut at night. Also, there may be a provision for the termination of the public right to use a walkway in its creation agreement, which is in conflict with the common law definition of a highway. Nevertheless, for the practical purposes of the trip and slip litigator, walkways can be treated as highways in most instances.

  Town centre or shopping centre "pedestrianised" spaces may be walkways (section 35 HA 1980 applies) or they may be footpaths (see next).

- **footpaths** – section 329[1] of the Highways Act 1980 provides that these are highways which carry only a public right of way on foot. They must be distinguished from footways, which form part of a carriageway highway.

- **public paths and bridleways** – these are both highways for trip and slip purposes. See section 66(1) of the Wildlife and Countryside Act 1981 and section 329(1) of the Highways Act 1980 for more detail, and for some minor categories of non-carriageway highways of little contemporary relevance.

Public Use

Although use may be restricted to certain classes of traffic, the public at large ("Her Majesty's subjects") must have a right to use a way before it becomes a highway. If one finds any restriction so far as public use is concerned – no matter how minor – then one is dealing with a private right of way, not a highway. Churchways provide a good examples of this – these are ways over which parishioners of a church have, usually through immemorial custom, acquired the right to pass. They are not highways.[15]

Creation

Creation of a highway at common law requires "dedication and acceptance". Putting it simply, the public accepts the landowner's dedication of the land to it. Dedication may be express or implied. Deciding whether or not there has been a dedication is a matter of fact. Dedication requires a permanent surrender of part of the landowner's dominium. Permanent means just that – once created, the public use can only be removed by operation of law.[16] In deciding whether there has been a dedication, one must differentiate between the public's permissive use of a way, and use of that way as of right. For example, the public may have had access to a particular way only by virtue of the landowner's acquiescence. If that acquiescence may be withdrawn at any time then the way is not a highway. Alternatively, the landowner might originally have had the right to withdraw acquiescence to public access, but may have lost it over time. In this latter instance, the way *is* a highway.

Section 31(1) of the Highways Act 1980 provides:

> "Where a way over any land, other than a way of such a character that use of it by the public could not give rise at common law to any presumption of dedication, has actually been enjoyed by the public as of right and without interruption for a full period of 20 years, the way is

---

15 Over time however most if not all churchways have become highways through dedication and acceptance. This is true for many other private rights of way also.

16 A possible exception may be found where there has been physical destruction of the land over which the highway ran.

deemed to have been dedicated as a highway unless there is sufficient evidence that there was no intention during that period to dedicate it."

Note however that although this section refers to a period of 20 years there is at common law no actual specified length of "time of use" required – even a few years may suffice if unequivocal evidence of intent to dedicate can be demonstrated. Section 31(9) provides that nothing in the section

> "...operates to prevent the dedication of a way as a highway being presumed on proof of user for any less period than 20 years, or being presumed or proved immediately before the commencement of this Act."

The erection of a notice by the landowner informing the public that there is no right of way, provided the notice remains *in situ*, will rebut the presumption created by 20 years of use (provided the notice was erected and remained in position during that period).

Dedication for a limited type of use is permissible (for example, on horseback only or on foot only) but not for a limited class of user. If a way is dedicated to a particular section of the public – say, members of a church – then a highway is not created. However, restrictions cannot be imposed subsequent to dedication.

Acceptance is easy to identify. Just ask "does the public use the way?" If the answer is in the affirmative then acceptance is present.

Highways may be created by statute. Section 24 of the Highways Act 1980 gives the Secretary of State for Transport, or any Highway Authority, power to build a new road. The construction of the new road must be complete before dedication and acceptance can be assumed to have taken place. The general rule is that until such a road links two existing highways and is surfaced such that it is passable by the public it is not yet a highway.

Section 26 of the Highways Act 1980 gives a County or District Council power to make a Public Path Creation Order and submit it to the Secretary of State for confirmation.

Section 30 of the Highways Act 1980 is a little used section, but allows for agreements between a landowners and a council for dedication of a highway. Under this section the public does not have to "accept" highways so created – indeed, such a highway would exist even if there has never been any user whatsoever. The Highway

Authority may not be responsible for the maintenance of such highways, and this can be a trap for the trip and slip litigator.

Section 38 of the Highways Act 1980 provides for agreements between builders of new housing or commercial estates and a Highway Authority. Section 38 Agreements generally set out the preconditions on which the Highway Authority will take over the maintenance of the roads in the new development once they have been constructed. Section 38(6) provides that agreements may contain such provisions

> "as to the dedication as a highway of any road or way to which the Agreement relates, the bearing of the expenses of the construction, maintenance or improvement of any highway, road, bridge or viaduct to which the Agreement relates and other relevant matters as the Authority making the Agreement thinks fit."

It is possible for a developer not to enter into a Section 38 Agreement and to simply build a road and give notice of intention to dedicate the road as a highway. In such case, section 37 provides that the local council (being the Highway Authority) can apply to the Magistrates' Court for an order declaring that it does not have to adopt the road as a highway on the grounds that it will not be of sufficient utility to the public to justify its being maintained at the public expense.

In the absence of a Section 38 Agreement, if the council purports to accept the dedication but does not give the necessary certification:

- that the road was made up in a satisfactory manner; or

- that it was kept in repair for the required twelve month period after dedication; or

- that it has been used as a highway during the twelve month period after dedication

then it does not become a highway maintainable at the public expense. In such case the developer can appeal to the Magistrates' Court, which has the power to order that the road should be so maintainable.

Miscellaneous

It is only the surface of land which constitutes the highway. The landowner can tunnel beneath a highway, for example, without restriction, provided support to the surface is maintained.

Highways exist regardless of ownership of the land over which they pass – that is, the category of owner has no bearing on whether or not a highway in fact exists.

A street is not always a highway. Some of the essential elements set out above may well be missing so far as a street is concerned. A "street" so far as the New Roads and Street Works Act 1991 is concerned is "the whole or any part of a highway, road, lane, footway, alley, passage, square, court or other land laid out as a way, whether it is a thoroughfare or not."

A railway is not a highway. The right to use a railway flows from the contract to travel on a train, operated by a company which in turn has a contractual right to travel along the railway track.

The public does not have a general right to use towpaths alongside canals or rivers, although rights may have been acquired by implication.

The foreshore, which is the area between the usual high and low water marks, is not a highway. That may seem obvious, but in point of fact there have been successful tripping cases brought in negligence against local authorities for accidents on beaches,[17] so it is thought worth mentioning here.

So far as bridges (or tunnels) are concerned, where one has a highway at either end of that bridge or tunnel, then the trip and slip litigator may safely treat the bridge or tunnel as part of that highway. Section 328(2) of the Highways Act 1980 says

> "Where a highway passes over a bridge or through a tunnel, that bridge or tunnel is to be taken for the purposes of this Act to be part of the highway."

See also *Gravesham BC v British Railways Board*[18] in relation to public ferries being highways.

---

17 See Occupiers' Liability later, and, for an unsuccessful foreshore case, *B (A Minor) v Thanet DC*, Canterbury CC judgment May 7, 1998 unreported.

18 *Gravesham BC v British Railways Board* [1978] Ch 379.

For a highway to exist there must be an identifiable route to be followed. A "right to roam" over land generally does not create a highway. For an illustration of this concept in practice, see the right of access to common land created by the Law of Property Act 1925.

Highway Authority Definitions

Highway authority terminology may differ somewhat from the foregoing. The Institution of Highways & Transportation's 2001 *Code of Practice* (see Chapters Five and Six later) suggests that local authorities should use the following definitions:

- The term "carriageway" is used for facilities used by motor vehicles.

- The term "footway" is used for segregated surfaced facilities used by pedestrians. Where these are not immediately adjoining a carriageway the term "remote footway" is used.

- The term "housing footway" is used for those footways serving predominantly housing areas, which may be unadopted as highways, but maintained by the authority as part of its housing function.

- The term "footpath" is retained for other forms of public rights of way.

- The term "cycleway" is used as the collective term for all segregated facilities used by cyclists.

- The term "running surface" is used as the collective term for all hardened surfaces within the highway including carriageways, footways and cycleways.

- The term "pavement" is used as the collective term for the construction of all running surfaces, particularly carriageways.

- The term "highway" is used to include "road" or "street".

- The term "authority" is used to include all forms of national and local authority having responsibility for highway maintenance.

Duty to Maintain

Is there someone or some body with a duty to maintain this highway? This is usually the first question a personal injury lawyer will want to ask when presented with a slip or trip scenario on what appears to be a highway. This is because in practice **the correct defendant will usually be the legal entity charged with the duty to repair the highway** concerned. Accordingly, we now move on to consider maintenance as a topic in itself.

CHAPTER 4
Maintenance

Maintenance

Highway Authority

In practice most slips and trips occurring on highways will be on highways maintained by public authority. As mentioned above the statutory definition in section 328 of the Highways Act 1980 is less than helpful. However, section 36 of the act is more useful. It defines what we are interested in – "a highway maintainable at the public expense". Such highways, fortunately, make up by far the largest category of highways.

Firstly, section 36(1) provides that, absent some subsequent event, all highways which were maintainable at public expense under the Highways Act 1959 remain such highways.

Secondly, section 36(2) sets out five types of highway which are maintainable at the public expense as follows:

(a) a highway constructed by a Highway Authority, otherwise than on behalf of some other person who is not a Highway Authority

(b) a highway constructed by a council within their own area under Part II of the Housing Act 1985, other than one in respect of which the local Highway Authority are satisfied that it has not been properly constructed, and a highway constructed by a council outside their own area under the said Part II, being, in the later case, a highway the liability of maintain which is, by virtue of the said Part II, vested in the council who are the local Highway Authority for the area in which the highway is situated;

(c) a highway that is a trunk road or a special road;

(d) a highway, being a footpath or bridle way, created in consequence of a public path creation order or a public path diversion order or in consequence of an order made by the Minister of Transport or the Secretary of State under section 247 of the Town and Country Planning Act 1990 or by a competent authority under section 257 of the Act, or dedicated in pursuance of a public path creation agreement; or a highway order, or of an order made under section 14 or 16 of the Harbours Act 1964, or of an order made under section 1 or 3 of the Transport and Works Act 1992.

Section 37 provides for adoption of a highway so as to become a highway maintainable at the public expense, notice having being served on the highway authority by the highway owner. Section 38 contains provisions for adoption by agreement. Section 228 provides that a highway authority may give notice of intention to adopt a highway as being a highway maintainable at the public expense where improvement works are intended to be carried out to a private road.

Note that highway authorities and the Minister can delegate their maintenance obligations to other public bodies. On this point, see sections 5, 6 and 8 of the Highways Act 1980 and also section 101 of the Local Government Act 1972.

To Whom Is the Duty Owed?

The duty is owed to members of the public. The public is all those who use the highway for the purposes of passage. It is owed to all persons who might be affected by breach of the duty. It must have been reasonably foreseeable that such persons might have been affected. For example, in *Haley* v *London Electricity Board*[19] it was held that it was held that a blind person's use of the highway in question was reasonably foreseeable and that the authority was liable for injury resulting from the blind claimant's trip over an obstruction placed by them.

Steps to maintain

In order to decide, where it may be in issue, whether a road or other way is a highway for which a public authority is responsible the best course of action is to try to establish whether the authority had ever taken steps to maintain it in the past. If it can be shown that they have done so then there is a strong argument that it is in fact such a highway.

If the highway is one which is maintained at the public expense then section 41(1) of the Highways Act 1980 is the section we must look at. This provides that the highway authority for such a highway is under

---

19 *Haley* v *London Electricity Board* [1965] AC 778.

a duty – statutory, by definition – to maintain the highway. It follows as a natural consequence that this highway authority will be the correct defendant in cases where failure to maintain is alleged.

Register of Maintainable Highways

Section 36(6) and (7) of the Highways Act 1980 provides:

- that local authorities must keep a list of all highways which are maintainable at the public expense
- which is to be available for inspection at all reasonable hours
- there is to be no charge for inspection

Note that the entirety of a highway which appears on the register may not be maintainable. For example, in urban areas the full length of a particular street may not be publicly maintainable.

Identity of the highway authority

There are a number of possible highway authorities:

- The **Secretary of State for Transport** is the highway authority for trunk roads and any roads constructed by that Department of State. The Highways Act 1980 section 6(1) allows the Secretary of State to delegate the responsibility for the maintenance of such roads to a local authority.

- **County councils** and **metropolitan district councils** will be the highway authority in their areas in most cases, except for the highways where the Secretary of State is the highway authority.

- In London the highway authority will be the **Council of a Borough** or the **Common Council of the City of London**.

- **District councils** (non-metropolitan), **parish or community councils** may in some cases (their having undertaken the duty, or made representations to do so to the highway authority) be responsible for the maintenance of highways within their district. Note that maintenance by a parish or community council does not absolve the highway authority of its duty.

- **Concessionaires** of toll roads under section 2 of the New Roads and Street Works Act 1991 are for our purposes the highway authority (note that the entity which would otherwise have been the highway authority may exercise the functions of the highway authority in an emergency).

Who is the proper defendant?

If the slip or, more usually, the trip, was caused by failure to repair, and the highway is not one which no one is liable to repair, then the appropriate defendant is obviously the authority or entity liable to maintain the highway in question.

If responsibility for repair lies with the Secretary of State, a county council or other local authority it is generally a reasonably straightforward matter.

Privately Repairable Highways

Individuals and bodies corporate may be liable for the repair of some highways by tenure, prescription or statute. There are conflicting authorities on whether liability to repair makes these individuals or bodies liable for personal injuries caused by failure to repair in itself, but in practice cases can usually be grounded in negligence, nuisance or on statute (such as the Occupiers' Liability Acts)

Contractors

In some instances a defendant other than the authority may be the appropriate party against whom proceedings should be issued, even where the highway is one which that authority is liable to maintain. An example would be where a contractor was doing work on the highway and a party suffers injury due to an occurrence in the course of that work. Here the difficulty is that the appropriate defendant may be either that contractor, or the highway authority. The correct defendant is selected in this instance as follows:

The proper defendant is the highway authority

Where the cause of action is the contractor's failure to carry out the work required to fulfil the highway authorities responsibility, in which case the authority remains responsible.

It is no defence on the part of authority to show that it instructed the contractor to do the work required and that the contractor negligently failed to do so (see *Hardaker* v *Idle*[20]).

The proper defendant is the contractor

Where there is negligence on the part of the contractor, while carrying out the works, but which negligence is not directly related to the authorities duties (say, an employee of the contractor spills something on which a pedestrian slips).

Statutory Undertakers

Alternatively, **a statutory undertaker** may be the appropriate defendant. There were statutory codes under the Public Utilities Street Works Act 1950 which regulated 'statutory undertakers'; however they are now regulated by the New Roads and Street Works Act 1991. Examples of statutory undertakers are telephone, water, electricity and gas suppliers. Their work is not maintenance. Works on "streets" are governed by the provisions of the 1991 Act.

A "street" is the whole or any part of:

- any highway, road, lane, footway, alley or passage

- any square or court

- any land laid out as a way, whether it is for the time being formed as a way or not.

---

20 *Hardaker* v *Idle* DC 1 QB 335(CA).

It does not matter whether the street forms part of a thoroughfare, nor does it have to be a highway maintainable at the public expense, to be covered by the 1991 Act.

The Act applies to "street works". These are defined, further to s. 48 of the 1991 Act, not as works for road purposes but rather are works carried out in a street and which involve the

> "placement, inspection, maintenance, adjustment, repair, alteration, renewal, removal or change of position of apparatus"

or are works required for or incidental to any such works.

The Act is an enabling act which sets out the duties of "Street Authorities" to co-ordinate and regulate works carried out in the highway by any organisation, and gives effect to a series of Regulations and Codes of Practice. These Codes, which recently have been reviewed, deal with:

- Specifications for the reinstatement of openings in highways
- Measures necessary when apparatus is affected by major works
- Safety at road works and street works
- Co-ordination of streetworks
- Inspections
- Record keeping

The 2001 Code says that the "New Roads and Street Works Act 1991, is an enabling Act setting out the duties of Street Authorities to co-ordinate and regulate works carried out in the highway by any organisation, and gives effect to a series of Regulations and Codes of Practice." It points out the requirement under the NRSWA 1991 for a highway authority to maintain information for the purposes of:

- Identifying streets described as traffic sensitive where work should be avoided at certain times of the day;

- Identifying structures under or over the street which need special consideration when work is planned;

- Identifying reinstatement categories used by statutory undertakers in the reinstatement of their street works.

This information, in particular under the last category, can be useful to the tripping and slipping litigator.

Street Works Licence

Street works, pursuant to section 51 of the 1991 Act, require either a Street Works licence or a statutory right to be carried out.

Street Works Register

A Street Works Register must be kept by the street authority. This register must:

- be made available for inspection
- be free of charge
- be available at reasonable times

The register is often a useful source of information in tripping cases resulting from street works. It will:

- identify the contractors
- identify the location of the works
- specify the type of works involved

The works must be carried out with reasonably practicable dispatch, and must be supervised by an appropriately qualified person.

Breaking Open and Making Good

Under the 1991 Act statutory undertakers have powers to break open the highway and, naturally, they have a concurrent duty to make good. If something laid under the highway by a statutory undertaker causes a defect at the surface, should proceedings be brought against the authority or the statutory undertaker? Such questions often arise in slip and trip scenarios – the only answer is to examine the duty of the authority and to establish whether it carried it out such with reasonable diligence. If it did not then the authority is usually the appropriate defendant, although concurrent liability is possible. The usual scenario here is failure to properly return a pavement after breaking it open – the statutory contractor's failure is no defence as far as the highway authority's breach of duty is concerned. Insofar as reinstatement is concerned section 70 of the 1991 Act applies. It provides, *inter alia*, for reinstatement as "soon after the completion of any part of the street works as is reasonably practicable and shall carry on and complete the reinstatement with all such dispatch as is reasonably practicable". There are very specific provisions in this section, such as:

- confirmation of reinstatement before the end of the next working day after completion
- prescription of materials and workmanship
- prescription of standards

Apportionment of Liability with Statutory Undertakers

In *Nolan v Merseyside County Council and Another*[21] the claimant tripped in a hole in the pavement where a fire hydrant cover was missing. The hydrant was owned by North West Water Authority. The Court of Appeal held that both the highway authority and the water authority were liable, the former being in breach of its duty to maintain the highway, and the latter liable for a failure to carry out necessary works of maintenance or repair as required by the Water Act 1945. The court apportioned the liability on a 50/50 basis, saying

> "if one remembers that the Plaintiff was entitled to succeed against each of the Defendants in this case on the ground of a breach by each of them respectively of an absolute statutory duty without otherwise any moral or legal "fault" or turpitude on either side, then we do not see how one can differentiate in any way between their several "responsibilities" for the Plaintiff's damage."

---

21 *Nolan v Merseyside County Council and Another*, unreported, 15 July 1982.

CHAPTER 5
Statutory Duty to Maintain

Statutory Duty to Maintain

Section 41

Under the provisions of section 41(1) of the Highways Act 1980, if the highway in question is a highway maintainable at the public expense, then the highway authority which is responsible for that maintenance is the correct defendant in any action arising out of an accident caused by a failure to maintain.

The provision of section 41(1) is that the

> "... authority who are for the time being the highway authority for a highway maintainable at the public expense are under a duty... to maintain the highway."

In *Rider* v *Rider*[22] it was held that this duty is "reasonably to maintain and repair the highway so that it is free of danger to all users who use the highway in the way normally to be expected of them". The case involved disrepair at the edge of a road. The edge was uneven and led onto mud and grass verges. The Court of Appeal held that the condition was foreseeably dangerous to reasonable drivers. It should be noted however, that the Court held that whether part of a highway is dangerous is a question of fact to be decided by the judge in each particular case.

What then is the extent of this duty "reasonably to maintain and repair"? In *Haydon* v *Kent County Council*[23] it was said that the ordinary meaning of 'maintain" was to:

> "keep something in existence in a state which enables it to serve the purpose for which it exists. In the case of a highway that purpose is to provide a means of for pedestrians or vehicles or both (according to the character of the highway). To keep that purpose intact involves more than repairing or keeping in repair."

---

22 *Rider* v *Rider* [1973] QB 505, [1973] 1 All ER 294.
23 *Haydon* v *Kent County Council* [1978] QB 343.

Haydon, being a 1978 case, pre-dates section 41(1). However, the claim was brought under section 41(1)'s predecessor, section 44(1) of the Highways Act 1959 which is accepted as being identical in effect.

The House of Lords decision in the winter case *Goodes v East Sussex County Council*[24] has been spoken of by some as have "overturned" *Haydon*. That would be very much overstating the situation. *Goodes* has indeed made life much more difficult for personal injury litigators where winter accidents are concerned. But it has not really had a major effect on the every day application of section 41(1). Section 41(1) still imposes an absolute duty, there is no doubt of that. What this means in practice is that the usual burden of proof is simply shifted from the claimant to the defendant. In *Goodes* Lord Clyde said:[25]

> "...The scheme of the provisions is in its broad effect that the authority should be liable for damage caused by a failure to take reasonable care to maintain a highway, but the injured party is not required to prove the failure to take reasonable care. It is for the authority to prove that it has exercised all reasonable care. Such a reversal of the onus which would have been imposed on the plaintiff in an action for damages at common law is justifiable by the consideration that the plaintiff is not likely to know or be able readily to ascertain in what respects the authority has failed in its duty. All that the plaintiff will know is that there is a defect in the road which has caused him injury and it is reasonable to impose on the authority the burden of explaining that they have exercised all reasonable care and should not be found liable."

So what *does* "maintain" mean in practice? The "strikingly unhelpful"[26] section 329(1) of the Highways Act 1980 provides that maintenance includes repair. What it says is that the term "maintenance" includes "repair" and the words "maintain" and "maintainable" are to be construed accordingly. This does not help much, indeed. However, one can say without fear of contradiction that there must be a *failure* to maintain or a *failure* to repair for there to be a breach of section 41. In practice considering what in fact constitutes "lack of repair" or "lack of maintenance" can be the most useful approach. After *Goodes* it is clear that the duty extends only to maintenance of the actual fabric of a highway. Futhermore, there is no

---

24 *Goodes v East Sussex County Council* [2000] 1 W.L.R. 1356.
25 [2000] 1 W.L.R. 1356 at 1368.
26 So described by Peter Edwards, Barrister in his article *"The Duty to Maintain Highways – Seasonal Cheer from the House of Lords"*, [2000] JPIL Issue 4/00 at 228.

duty to improve a highway *per se*. However, a highway authority may be negligent if it fails to exercise its power to improve (in cases, for example, where there has been a considerable increase in traffic). If a highway authority does "improve" it needs to make sure that it does not in fact make matters worse. In *Duffill v South Somerset DC*, a county court unreported case, the claimant slipped and fell on a road used as a public path, for which the highway authority was responsible. Following complaints made over a number of years, works were carried out. Steps were built which turned out not to be consistent with use by horses or motorcycles. Accordingly, further works were carried out by removing every alternate, or two out of three, retaining strips, which had created the steps, and grading the path. No attempt was made to compact the soil. After completion of the works by a contractor, no attempt was made by the highway authority to inspect. The soil was sandy soil. Seven days after the works were completed, a witness wrote to the highway authority stating that while the earth was dry there was no real problem in gaining a foothold but that rain would turn the ramp into a slide. The danger was that walkers would find themselves sliding from top to bottom. In due course the claimant slipped and fell, causing herself injury. Held, for the claimant, that on the facts the road was a danger on the date of the accident, some seven weeks after the work was completed. The action of the highway authority in removing the steps was a partial failure to maintain in that it created a hazard. The state of the path after the "improvements" was far worse than beforehand. There was no statutory defence available under the Highways Act 1980 section 58.

Repair & Maintenance – Standards

Highways must be in a fit state for ordinary traffic. In *Sharpness New Docks and Gloucester and Birmingham Navigation Co v Attorney-General*[27] it was said that

> "it is the duty of road authorities to keep their public[28] highways in a state fit to accommodate the ordinary traffic which passes or may be expected to pass along them."

---

27 *Sharpness New Docks and Gloucester and Birmingham Navigation Co v Attorney-General* [1915] AC 654.
28 "Public" is redundant as there can be no such thing as a private highway.

Ascertaining more precisely what this 'state fit' is can only be done by making reference to other cases.

Those which relate to parts of pavement standing proud to a greater or lesser degree are very useful here. The "Liverpool Trilogy"[29] are the best known of these cases. A highway is not to be criticised to the standards of a bowling green – in *Littler* it was said:

> "The test in relation to a length of pavement is reasonable foreseeability of danger. A length of pavement is only dangerous if, in the ordinary course of human affairs, danger may reasonably be anticipated from its continued use by the public who usually pass over it. It is a mistake to isolate and emphasise a particular difference in levels between flagstones unless that difference is such that a reasonable person who noticed and considered it would regard it as presenting a real source of danger. Uneven surfaces and differences in level between flagstones of about an inch may cause a pedestrian to trip and stumble, but such characteristics have to be expected."

This passage gives a good idea of courts attitude to want of repair. It is a succinct statement of the law on this question. However, the reference to a difference of about one inch being expected is not always followed in other cases. In *Griffiths*, for example, a rocking paving slab giving rise to a half-inch projection was held at first instance to be dangerous. The point wasn't taken on the appeal, which deal with the statutory defence. However Sellers LJ said:

> "We are all of us accustomed to walk on uneven and irregular surfaces and we can all of us trip on cobblestones, cat's-eyes, studs marking pedestrian crossings, as well as other projections. If the finding that the half-inch projection of a solitary flagstone in a wide pavement has to be accepted because of the technicalities of this case, as my brethren think, I have perhaps said enough to indicate that it is a standard which in my view should not become a precedent or guide in ordinary circumstances."

In *Meggs* the highway authority had regarded a tripping hazard of ¾ of an inch as not being dangerous (although they did carry out repairs after the accident). In the Court of Appeal, which agreed with the highway authority's view, Lord Denning MR said:

> "It seems to me, using ordinary knowledge of pavements, that everyone must take account of the fact that there may be unevenness here or there.

---

[29] *Giffiths v Liverpool Corporation* [1966] 1 WLR 467; *Meggs v Liverpool Corporation* [1968] 1 WLR 689; *Littler v Liverpool Corporation* [1968] 2 All ER 343.

There may be a ridge of half an inch or three quarters of an inch occasionally, but that is not the sort of thing which makes it dangerous or not reasonably safe."

In *Mills v Barnsley Metropolitan Borough Council*[30] Steyn LJ said:

"... I add that in drawing the inference of dangerousness in this case the Judge impliedly set a standard which if generally used in the thousands of tripping cases which come before the courts every year, would impose an unreasonable burden upon the Highway Authorities in respect of minor depressions and holes in streets which in a less than perfect world the public must simply regard as a fact of life. It is important that our tort laws should not impose unreasonably high standards..... This branch of the law of tort ought to represent a sensible balance or compromise between private and public interests."

Notwithstanding *Meggs* and *Griffiths* (or indeed *Mills*), slip and trip litigators need to always remember that the reference to *'differences in levels...of about one inch'* in *Littler* does not mean that smaller differences will ensure that a personal injury claim will fail.

For example, in *Pitman v Southern Electricity Board*[31] it was held that a projection of one-eight of an inch was sufficient to enable the claimant to succeed.

On the other hand, in the unreported case of *Lawman v Waltham Forest London Borough Council*[32] a 20mm (i.e. just over ¾ inch) hazard was found not to be a failure to maintain.

In *Hartley v Burnley BC*[33] an area of pavement where flagstones changed to tarmac was held to be dangerous notwithstanding the lack of any defined trip as such. Some tarmac had broken off, and some tarmac had different textures (part was ridged and part was uneven), and that was found to be sufficient. The street was a high pedestrian volume location and was steep.

---

30 *Mills v Barnsley Metropolitan Borough Council* [1992] PIQR 291.
31 *Pitman v Southern Electricity Board* [1978] 3 All ER 901.
32 *Lawman v Waltham Forest London Borough Council*, unreported, 23 January 1980, CA.
33 *Hartley v Burnley BC* [1996] CLY 5670.

"Fit State"

The general principles a court will use to decide whether a highway is in a fit state, which is to say, reasonably safe, are fairly easy to identify and may be summarised as follows:

- there must be reasonable foreseeability of danger;

- minor irregularities do not render highways legally unsafe;

- a question of whether a particular highway is unsafe is one for the trial judge to decide;

- courts have declined to make declarations, in terms of precise size of irregularity, as to what constitutes an unsafe highway;

- differences in level of one inch or more are likely to be found unsafe;

- it is uncertain whether the carriageway of roads must be as safe for pedestrians as the pavement;

- there are hierarchies of roads which may be maintained to different standards (e.g. a rural footpath is not expected to be maintained to the standard of an urban pavement);

- trivial defects may give rise to liability if suddenly and unexpectedly created.

Highway Authority Maintenance Practice

Practically speaking, the best way of showing that a highway is unsafe is to show that the highway authority's own standards were not complied with. Where are those standards to be found? The July 2001 *Code of Practice for Maintenance Management (Delivering Best Value in Highway Maintenance)* [34] – the 2001 Code – which is available from the Institution of Highways & Transportation [35] is the best source of information. (However, see also *Local Authority Liability* [36] (Morrell

---

34 DETR 2001, ISBN 0 902933 37 X.
35 IHT, 6 Endsleigh Street, London WC1H ODZ.
36 *Local Authority Liability*, Morrell J & Foster R eds., Jordans 1998.

& Foster, eds.) for an interesting treatment of highway liability from the perspective of the defendant.)

The 2001 Code was developed as a project by officers of UK national, devolved, and local governments. The concept was to encourage "co-ordination and consistency in the delivery of local highway maintenance services and to facilitate sharing of developing best practice". The suggested recommendations of the 2001 Code are explicitly not mandatory on authorities. However the 2001 Code notes that highway authorities have certain legal obligations with which they need to comply, and which may be the subject of claims or legal action by those seeking to establish non–compliance by authorities. The 2001 Code states:

> It has been recognised that in such cases, the contents of this Code of Practice may be considered to be a relevant consideration. In these circumstances, where authorities elect in the light of local circumstances to adopt policies, procedures or standards differing from those suggested by the 2001 Code, **it is essential for these to be identified together with the reasoning for such differences** (*emphasis added*).

The main point made here is that the 2001 Code establishes best practice. If a highway authority does not meet the standards laid down, it should say why not.

The 2001 Code goes on to say:

> There has also been in recent years a general increase in the tendency for users to pursue claims against authorities where injury or damage has occurred and they consider there has been a failure on the part of the authority to maintain the highway to required standards. In the light of this trend **the need is stressed, throughout this Code, for authorities to establish and publish clear policies, and maintain consistent detailed regimes of inspection, repair, recording and monitoring** (*emphasis added*).

In brief, stripping out the earnest references to focusing "on the needs of users" and retaining "reasonable diversity consistent with local choice", the 2001 Code's objectives are:

- To encourage the development, adoption and regular review of policies for highway maintenance;

- To encourage harmonisation of highway maintenance practice and standards;

- To encourage the adoption of an efficient and consistent approach in the collection, processing and recording of highway inventory, highway condition;

- To encourage the adoption and regular review of a risk management regime in the determination of local technical and operational standards.

The 2001 Code should be used by authorities "as a benchmark".

The 2001 Code states that highway maintenance is a "wide ranging function" and includes the following types of activity:

- Network Safety
- Complying with statutory obligations
- Meeting users' needs
- Network Serviceability
- Ensuring availability
- Achieving integrity
- Maintaining reliability
- Enhancing quality
- Network Sustainability
- Minimising cost over time
- Maximising value to the community
- Maximising environmental contribution.

The 2001 Code goes on to state that "within each of these types of maintenance there are various maintenance activities". The maintenance activities of most interest to the tripping and slipping litigator are headed Reactive, Routine and Programmed.

Reactive

This is in response to inspections, complaints or emergencies:

- All elements – sign and make safe
- All elements – provide initial temporary repair
- All elements – provide permanent repair

Routine

This is a regular consistent schedule for patching, cleaning, landscape maintenance and other activities. Examples include:

- Carriageways, footways and cycleways – minor works and patching
- Drainage Systems – cleansing and repair
- Fences and barriers – repair
- Traffic signs and bollards – cleansing and repair
- Road markings and studs – replacement
- Lighting Installations – cleansing and repair

Programmed

Planned schemes, primarily of resurfacing, reconditioning or reconstruction:

- Carriageways – minor works, resurfacing or reconstruction
- Footways – minor works, resurfacing or reconstruction
- Cycleways – minor works, resurfacing or reconstruction

There are three other heads – Regulatory, Weather and Other Emergencies and Winter Service.

The 2001 Code says that "policies, priorities and programmes for highway maintenance should be formally approved and adopted by authorities". They should be published and incorporated into a Highway Network Management Plan and the Local Transport Plan.

The 2001 Code also notes the crucial importance of a clear understanding of the powers and duties of a highway authority. It notes such authorities have a general duty of care to users and the community to maintain the highway in a condition fit for its purpose. It states:

> "This [duty of care] should be applied to all decisions affecting policy, priority, programming and implementation of highway maintenance works."

Highway Maintenance Statutory Duties – The 2001 Code's Viewpoint

The 2001 Code identifies a number of specific pieces of legislation relating to Highway Maintenance, from a highway authority's perspective. The main legislation noted, naturally, is the Highways Act 1980. It says section 41 should be noted in particular as imposing "a duty to maintain highways maintainable at public expense, and almost all claims against authorities relating to highway functions arise from the alleged breach of this Section."

On section 41 the 2001 Code notes that the legal judgment in the case of *Goodes* v *East Sussex*

> "indicates that there is no duty on local highway authorities to remove ice from highways under the general responsibility to "maintain the highway" in Section 41....It is important to note however that this judgement does not remove liability in all circumstances, for example where ice has formed from water standing on the running surface resulting from defective or poorly maintained drainage."

The 2001 Code's view of *Goodes* is that

> "the judgment suggests that the maintenance duty under Section 41 of the Act relates only to the "highway fabric" and **therefore has potentially wider implications** (*emphasis added*) than for winter service, which will evolve over time."

The 2001 Code notes that section 150 of the Act imposes a duty upon authorities to remove any obstruction of the highway resulting from "accumulation of snow or from the falling down of banks on the side of the highway, or from any other cause".

Note that the 2001 Code's commentary on the Local Authorities (Transport Charges) Regulations 1998 includes a brief reference "to the clearance of accident debris" – potentially a tripping matter.

The 2001 Code points out that the Highway Act duties sit within a wider statutory framework. That framework includes:

- Road Traffic Regulation Act 1984

- Traffic Signs and General Directions 1994

- Road Traffic Act 1988 (road safety issues)

- Road Traffic Reduction Act 1997

- Local Authorities (Transport Charges) Regulations 1998

- Transport Act 2000 (facilitates the introduction of rural road hierarchies).

- Health and Safety at Work Act 1974

- Management of Health and Safety at Work Regulations 1992

- Construction (Design and Management) Regulations 1994 (these last three provide for a requirement for highway authorities to carry out work in a safe manner and establish arrangements for the management of construction works).

There is "an increasing range of legislation regulating the environmental affects of [authorities] operations", including:

- Wildlife and Countryside Act 1981

- Environmental Protection Act 1990 (requirement to keep the highway clear of litter and refuse which for local roads is not a duty for the highway authority)

- Noxious Weeds Act 1959 (action to inhibit the growth and spread of injurious weeds growing within the highway. Weed spraying is also regulated by the Environment Agency. See also Health and Safety Commission Code of Practice.)

- Rights of Way Act 1990

- Countryside and Rights of Way Act 2000

Summary

The claimant must show that:

a. that the highway was not reasonably safe where the accident occurred (bearing in mind the "fit state principles" discussed above); and

b. the accident was caused by the dangerous condition of the highway.

There is no need to prove fault. Once a claimant succeeds in establishing a and b then the highway authority can only fall back on the statutory defence afforded by section 58 of the Highways Act 1980, with which we deal next.

CHAPTER 6

The Statutory Defence

The Statutory Defence

Background

One occasionally still reads of or hears reference to "misfeasance" and "nonfeasance" in discussions of highway liability. It is worth emphasising that the distinction is largely moot. The importance of distinguishing between the two arose from the position at common law where a highway authority was not liable for injury resulting from a failure to keep the highway in repair. That common law immunity did not apply to misfeasance (nor to improperly carried out repairs). The Highways Act 1959, section 44(1) was the original statute providing for a duty to maintain, but that piece of legislation kept the exemption for non-feasance. The position was firstly changed by the Highways (Miscellaneous Provisions) Act 1961, section 1(1) of which removed the exemption. The position is now as provided by section 41(1) of the Highways Act 1980, repeated here for ease of reference, which imposes on *"[t]he authority who are for the time being the highway authority for a highway maintainable at the public expense...a duty to maintain the highway."*

Remember, that while in an ordinary negligence action a claimant must prove a) that the defendant had been guilty of a lack of reasonable care and b) that such lack of reasonable care was the cause of the injury, in an action under the Highways Act a claimant does not have to prove either. It is up to the defendant to prove that it did take reasonable care. Only once it has proved this is the statutory defence available to it. On this point, see the judgement of Diplock LJ in *Griffiths v Liverpool Corporation.*[37]

---

37 *Griffiths v Liverpool Corporation* [1966] 2 All ER 1015, CA.

Defence

Section 58(1) of the Highways Act 1980 provides what is usually referred to as the "statutory defence" as follows:

> In an action against a highway authority in respect of damage resulting from their failure to maintain a highway maintainable at the public expense it is a defence (without prejudice to any other defence or the application of the law relating to contributory negligence) to prove that the authority had taken such care as in all the circumstances was reasonably required to secure that the part of the highway to which the action relates was not dangerous for traffic.

Relevant Factors

Under section 58(2) the court must take into account:

- the character of the highway

- the traffic reasonably expected to use it

- the standard of maintenance appropriate to such a highway

- the state of repair reasonable persons would expect

- the knowledge which the highway authority had (or reasonably should have had) of the dangerous condition

- the kind of warning notices displayed.

It is no defence to show that the authority had arranged for a competent person to carry out (or supervise) repairs to the highway unless the authority can show it gave that person proper instructions and that those instructions had been carried out.[38]

It will usually come down to a question as to whether the steps (because there will almost inevitably be some) taken by the authority were sufficient. Authorities have large numbers of highways within their area of responsibility; they have limited resources. This is accepted, and a court will attempt to establish two elements –

1) was there a system of inspection?

---

38 *Wentworth v Wiltshire C.C.* [1933] Q.B. 654.

and if so:

2) was this system reasonable in the circumstances?

In *Pridham* v *Hemel Hempstead Corporation*[39], the leading case of frequency of inspection, it was held that if the authority could establish that its system of inspection was in fact reasonable, and that despite it the fault occurred unbeknownst to them, they had discharged their duty under section 58. (However, see a more detailed commentary on *Pridham* below).

Appropriate System

An authority will not be able to rely on a system of inspection which suffices for a small country road as being reasonable for a busy main road – city centre pedestrianised areas, to give an example, should be inspected at approximately three-monthly intervals.

An authority must be able to show that not only did it carry out inspections, but that it also acted upon the reports of the inspectors. In this regard proper records are important.

When dealing with the statutory defence it is important to understand what the highway authority itself believes its duties to be, and in particular to know whether the system of inspection in question was appropriate or adequate. One must turn again to the 2001 Code to see how highway authorities' own "best practice" should operate. The tripping and slipping litigator can then check to see whether that has been followed in the particular instance, and, if not, will have a reasonable chance of ensuring that the highway authority fails to prove its case.

The 2001 Code – Statutory Defence matters

The 2001 Code says that in order to effectively defend claims for failure to maintain "the efficiency, accuracy and quality of information and records maintained by authorities will be crucial". The requirement to provide an initial response within 21 days "will need to

---

39 *Pridham* v *Hemel Hempstead Corporation* (1970) 114 SJ 884 (CA).

be informed by a view of the potential of the authority to defend a claim". The records should be compliant with the CPR standards of evidence. Record systems should include:

- all user contact information

- records of inspection

- records of condition

- records of all maintenance activity

These should be co–ordinated with other relevant record systems such as road accidents databases.

Records – Comprehensive, Accurate and Co-ordinated

The 2001 Code states that comprehensive and accurate records should be kept of all highway maintenance activities undertaken, particularly:

- safety inspections
- other inspections
- identifying the time of any response
- identifying the nature of any response.

The nature of any response should include:

- nil returns
- subsequent required follow up action.

Arrangements "should be established to ensure the effective co-ordination of all highway maintenance records with other relevant record systems, including road accident information, together with a programme for regular review".

Network Hierarchy

A hierarchy is "the foundation of a coherent, consistent and auditable maintenance strategy". The priorities and actual use of each road in a network must be reflected by its place in the hierarchy. The road's location will often determine the place in the hierarchy – rural, urban, busy shopping street, residential street and so on. Sometimes the purpose of a route will determine its place – a street leading to a university's main entrance, for example. There is potential for conflicting priorities. As an example of this, the 2001 Code notes that "footway priorities may sometimes conflict with carriageway priorities, and hence it is necessary to define separate footway and cycleway hierarchies".

The 2001 Code notes that hierarchies are dynamic. Therefore, they must be regularly reviewed

> "to reflect changes in network characteristics and use so that maintenance policies, practices, and standards reflect the actual use of the network rather than the use expected when the hierarchy was originally defined. Where major maintenance, construction or other development involves significant traffic diversion, or when congestion in one part of the network results in traffic shift to another part of the network, it is important that these changes are reflected in the hierarchy and subsequently in the maintenance regime".

Accordingly, the litigator must not simply accept an authority's statement of hierarchical position without further consideration of whether it was appropriate, both at the time of initial categorisation and at the time of the accident. The 2001 Code says that carriageway hierarchies should be designated "having regard to traffic flows but also on the basis of risk assessment and the role of the particular section of carriageway in the network". A litigator can legitimately ask an authority which raises a section 58 defence to confirm, with details, that that has been done.

Before a litigator can deal with a section 58 defence, which will be based on a claim that the inspection and maintenance regime carried out was appropriate and adequate for the highway in question, there must exist an understanding of the various categories in the usual highway authority hierarchy. Only then can a decision be made whether to challenge the hierarchy category chosen by the highway authority. As we will see later when we look at the inspection regime, frequency of inspection differs according to categorisation. Inspection frequency goes to the heart of the Section 58 defence. Accordingly, we next look at the hierarchy suggested in the 2001 Code.

Carriageway Hierarchy

The first few categories set out here are of limited importance in tripping and slipping scenarios but are included for the sake of completeness. The categories and descriptions here are taken directly from the 2001 Code, with only minor editing.

Category 1

These are Motorways, described as limited access routes for fast moving long distance motorway regulations traffic. They are fully grade separated and apply restrictions on use.

Category 2

These are Strategic Routes. These are sometimes called "Trunk" roads or Principal "A" routes between primary destinations. Typically, there is little frontage access or pedestrian traffic. Speed limits are usually in excess of 40 mph. There are few junctions. Pedestrian crossings are either segregated or controlled and parked vehicles are generally prohibited.

Category 3a

These are Main Distributors, otherwise termed "Major Urban Network" or "Inter-Primary Links". They carry short and medium distance traffic.

In urban areas speed limits are usually 40 mph or less, parking is restricted at peak times and there are measures for pedestrian safety.

Category 3b

These are Secondary Distributors, otherwise termed B and C Classified Roads. This category also incorporates unclassified urban bus routes. There is local traffic, frontage access and frequent junctions. In rural areas these roads link the larger villages and HGV generators to the

Strategic and Main Distributor Network. In built up areas these roads have 30 mph speed limits and very high levels of pedestrian activity with some crossing facilities including zebra crossings. On-street parking is generally unrestricted except for safety reasons

Category 4a

These are Link Roads linking between the Main and Secondary Distributor Network. There is frontage access. There are frequent junctions. In rural areas these roads link smaller villages to the distributor roads. They are of varying width and and not always capable of carrying two way traffic. In urban areas they are residential or industrial inter-connecting roads with 30 mph speed limits random pedestrian movements and uncontrolled parking

Category 4b

These are Local Access Roads. They serve limited numbers of properties carrying only access traffic. In rural areas these roads serve small settlements and provide access to individual properties and land. They are often only single lane width and unsuitable for HGVs. In urban areas they are often residential loop roads or *culs de sac*.

Footway Hierarchy

It is important to understand that footway maintenance standards should be "determined by pedestrian usage and not the importance of the road in the network". Factors to be taken into account include:

- age and distribution of the population

- proximity of schools

- proximity of other establishments attracting higher than normal numbers of pedestrians.

So far as categorisation is concerned the 2001 Code says the following should be taken into account:

- Pedestrian volume
- Usage and proposed usage
- Accident and other risk assessment
- Age and type of footway
- Character and traffic use of adjoining carriageway.

The suggested categories are:

Category 1a

These are termed Prestige Walking Zones. They are found in "Prestige Areas" in towns and cities with exceptionally high usage (e.g. Oxford Street in London).

Category 1

These are Primary Walking Routes. They are found in busy urban shopping and business areas. They are also main pedestrian routes linking interchanges between different modes of transport (e.g. between railways and underground stations or bus stops).

Category 2

These are Secondary Walking Routes, described as medium usage routes through local areas feeding into primary routes, local shopping centres, large schools, industrial centres and so on.

Category 3

These are Link Footways. They link local access footways through urban areas and busy rural footways.

Category 4

These are Local Access Footways, associated with low usage, short estate roads to the main routes and *culs de sac*.

There is also a Cycleway Hierarchy in the 2001 Code, not dealt with here.

Having an understanding of the categories we can proceed to look at the inspection regime.

Inspection Regime

The most crucial component of highway maintenance, according to the 2001 Code, is "the establishment of an effective regime of inspection, assessment and recording". Characteristics of an inspection regime are:

- frequency of inspection
- types of items to be recorded
- nature of response

The key objectives of highway maintenance, according to the 2001 Code, are network safety, network serviceability and network sustainability. The inspection regime should provide the basic information for addressing these. Systematic and consistent application of all aspects of the inspection regime are vital. The 2001 Code notes:

> "This is particularly important in the case of network safety, where information may be crucial in respect of legal proceedings. It is important to recognise however that all information recorded, even if not primarily intended for network safety purposes, may have consequential implications for safety and may therefore be relevant to legal proceedings".

Frequencies for Safety Inspections

The 2001 Code says these should be based on:

- Category within the network hierarchy
- Traffic use, characteristics and trends

- Incident and inspection history
- Characteristics of adjoining network elements
- Wider policy or operational considerations.

Other factors to be taken into account:

- Where road use is " at the margin of the category" but has higher than normal levels of growth.

- Where extensive development may be taking place or planned.

- Where there are higher than normal level of accidents or related incidents.

- Where traffic flow is low but there are high numbers of pedestrians.

- Where the route is the subject of promotion by the highway authority for example as a "Safer Route to School" or it provides access to, for example, a railway station.

Frequency of inspection is based upon network category. However, that is merely a starting point. The 2001 Code says that in defining a safety inspection regime authorities should take into account all of the above factors. In practice, what the litigation professional needs to look for in statutory defence situations are, firstly, instances where category is the *only* factor considered. Secondly, the correctness of the category assigned needs to be evaluated.

Summary of Inspection Regime

Highway	Category	Category No.	How often?
Roads	Strategic Route	2	1 month
	Main Distributor	3(a)	1 month
	Secondary Distributor	3(b)	1 month
	Link Road	4(a)	3 months
	Local access	4(b)	1 year
Footways	Prestige Area	1(a)	1 month
	Primary Walking Route	1	1 month
	Secondary Walking Route	2	3 months
	Link Footway	3	6 months
	Local Access Footway	4	1 year

As can be seen, frequency varies considerably. In a statutory defence situation therefore it is possible to attack the defence – always bearing in mind that the burden of proof is on the highway authority – by challenging the category, or the methodology used to assign the category. For an example of a case in which frequency of inspection was found to be inadequate see *Jacobs* v *Hampshire County Council*,[40] where the design of the road (cobbles abutting tarmac) made the road particularly susceptible to water penetration. In *Jacobs* the category was correct but other factors had not been taken into account.

---

40 *Jacobs* v *Hampshire County Council* (1984) *The Times*, May 28 (QBD).

Safety Inspection Procedures

The 2001 Code says "all observed defects that provide for any degree of risk to users should be recorded, irrespective of the likely level of response. The degree of deficiency in highway elements will be crucial in determining the nature and speed of response." It goes on to note:

- some general guidance can be given on the likely risk associated with particular defects but

- on-site judgement will always need to take account of particular circumstances.

As an example of the need for on-site judgement it cites the fact that the level of risk degree from a pothole "depends upon not merely its depth but also its surface area and location."

Defects observed during safety inspections are defined either as Category 1 or Category 2. Category 1 defects are of principal interest to trip and slip litigation professionals as they are defects which "require prompt attention because they represent an immediate or imminent hazard or because there is a risk of short-term structural deterioration." All other defects fall into Category 2.

If a defect is found what should the highway authority do? The 2001 Code says that Category 1 defects should be:

"corrected or made safe at the time of the Inspection, if reasonably practicable. In this context, making safe may constitute displaying warning notices, coning off or fencing off to protect the public from the defect. If it is not possible to correct or make safe the defect at the time of inspection, which will generally be the case, repairs of a permanent or temporary nature should be carried out as soon as possible **and in any case within a period of 24 hours** (*emphasis added*)."

Thereafter, permanent repair should be carried out within 28 days. Category 2 Defects should be repaired within planned programmes of work

"with priority depending on the degree of deficiency, traffic and site characteristics. These priorities should be considered, together with access requirements, other works upon the road network, traffic levels, and the need to minimise traffic management, in compiling the programmes of work."

The 2001 Code goes on to say that authorities:

- should adopt a range of local target response times

- apply them in responding to various categories of defect, according to

- the perceived degree of risk, having regard to

- the characteristics and use of the Network.

In *Pridham* it was held that the highway authority must show sufficiently careful consideration before adopting an inspection regime. It is submitted that the authority must show that it has taken into consideration the foregoing matters in order to demonstrate that it comes within the protection afforded by the statutory defence, or else be able to show good reason for not doing so. *Pridham* is based on a "reasonableness" test. If the highway authority can show the regime was reasonable (for example, by demonstrating that it followed the 2001 Code) then it is likely to make out the defence. Conversely, if it cannot show good reason for not following the 2001 Code then the claimant is in a stronger position. In *Pridham* the defect had developed a very short time before the accident, on a residential road quarterly inspected. The court found that although it would have been practicable to inspect more often it would not be reasonsable to require it, given the character of the road. However, the authority in *Pridham* was not called upon by the claimant (then, plaintiff) – or, indeed, by the court – to give any justification of category choice or inspection frequency. It is entirely possible that if the information in the 2001 Code had been available to the claimant then searching questions could have been asked, resulting in a different outcome.

CHAPTER 7
Snow and Ice

Snow and Ice

Maintenance in cold weather

The leading case used to be *Haydon* v *Kent CC*. The claimant there had slipped on an icy, steep footpath. In that case it was said that the duty to maintain could include "clearing snow and ice" or "providing temporary protection by gritting". Shaw LJ in Haydon said that the purpose of a highway was to provide a means of passage and

> "[t]o keep that purpose intact involves more than repairing or keeping in repair". He went on to say that there may be "extreme cases in special circumstances where a liability for failure to maintain not related to want of repair may arise. Such cases are not readily brought to mind although I would not wish to exclude them by confining the scope of maintenance to matters of repairing and keeping in repair."

Following *Haydon*, where snow and ice were concerned a failure to maintain must have incorporated an element of "fault" to be actionable in a slip and trip context. Catchwords in snow and ice cases were **fault, culpability**[41] and **blameworthiness**.[42]

The decision in *Goodes* has changed the law. In this case the claimant pursued an action under section 41(1) after his car skidded on ice and collided with a bridge. The House of Lords decided that:

> "A highway authority's duty under section 41(1) of the Highways Act, 1980, to maintain the highway was an absolute duty to keep the fabric of the highway in such good repair as to render its physical condition safe for ordinary traffic to pass at all seasons of the year, but it did not include a duty to prevent the formation of ice or remove the accumulation of snow on the road; and that accordingly, the highway authority was not in breach of its statutory duty and was not liable for the [claimant's] accident."

To put it another way, the dissenting judgement of Lord Denning in *Haydon* was found to be "completely convincing". The duty to

---

41 Shaw LJ in *Haydon* spoke of "a culpable breach".
42 See Boreham J in *Bartlett* v *Dept of Transport* (1985) *The Times*, 8 January.

maintain under section 44(1) of the 1959 Highways Act was stated to be the same duty as that which common law or statute imposed before the Act upon the inhabitants at large, or by succession, upon the previous highway authorities. If the previous duty to maintain did not include a duty to remove snow or ice – which it did not – then the duty under section 44(1) of the 1959 Act did not do so either. Following on from this, therefore, while a highway authority had an absolute duty under section 41(1) of the Highways Act 1980 to keep the fabric of the highway in a good state of repair so as to render it safe for ordinary traffic at all seasons of the year, that did not include a duty to do anything other than to remedy defects in the fabric of the highway. This part of the judgment suggests that the maintenance duty under section 41 of the Act relates only to the "highway fabric". It therefore has potentially wider implications than merely for snow and ice cases.

The 2001 Code firstly notes that *Goodes* indicates that there is no duty on local highway authorities to remove ice from highways under the general responsibility to "maintain the highway" in section 41 of the Highways Act 1980. It goes on to say, however, that:

> "It is important to note however that this judgment does not remove liability in all circumstances, for example where ice has formed from water standing on the running surface resulting from defective or poorly maintained drainage. There is also in Section 150 of the Act a duty upon authorities to remove any obstruction of the highway resulting from "accumulation of snow or from the falling down of banks on the side of the highway, or from any other cause".

The reference to section 150 needs further attention.

Section 150 of the 1980 Act

It should be first noted that in *Haydon* Lord Denning MR decided the matter fell outside the scope of that section 41(1), but came instead within the ambit of section 129 of the 1959 Act. Section 129 is the predecessor to section 150 of the Highways Act 1980.

Section 129 said:

> (1) If an obstruction arises in a highway from accumulation of snow or from the falling down of banks on the side of the highway, or from

> any other cause, the highway authority for the highway shall cause the obstruction to be removed from time to time......

Contrast this with section 150(1) below and we see that the words "from time to time" no longer appear.

In *Haydon* Denning said "[b]y no shadow of argument can [the duty] be called an absolute duty. Nor does it give rise to a civil action for damages if it is not performed." It seems that the words "from time to time" were sufficient for Denning to infer a discretion on the part of the authority. He said:

> "[section 129 of the 1959 Act] is very appropriate to deal with highways which get blocked or impeded by snow or ice...It puts on the highway authority a duty to remove the obstruction, but it leaves it to the highway authority to carry out that duty at such time as it thinks best. To do it "from time to time". They have, therefore, a discretion: save that, if they delay too long, they can be brought to book by a magistrate's order.

However section 150 of the Highways Act 1980 provides

> (1) If an obstruction arises in a highway from accumulation of snow or from the falling down of banks on the side of the highway, or from any other cause, the highway authority shall remove the obstruction.
>
> (2) If a highway authority fail to remove an obstruction which it is their duty under this section to remove, a magistrates' court may, on a complaint made by any person, by order require the authority to remove the obstruction within such period (not being less than 24 hours) from the making of the order as the court thinks reasonable, having regard to all the circumstances of the case.
>
> (3) In considering whether to make an order under this section, and if so, what period to allow for the removal of the obstruction, the court shall in particular have regard to
>
> > (a) the character of the highway to which the complaint relates, and the nature and amount of the traffic by which it is ordinarily used,
> >
> > (b) the nature and extent of the obstruction, and
> >
> > (c) the resources of manpower, vehicles and equipment for the time being available to the highway authority for work on highways and the extent to which those resources are being, or need to be, employed elsewhere by that authority on such work."

As already mentioned, the words "from time to time" have been removed.

Commentators have argued strongly, and it seems to be the case, that Denning meant the section did not ground a civil action **only** because it did not impose an absolute duty. Once more, it is clear that this lack of absolute duty was related to the words "from time to time". It therefore follows that the removal of these words, as in section 150, removes the discretionary element on the part of the authority also, and that as a consequence section 150 **would** ground a civil action for damages if the duty was not performed. The 2001 Code certainly accepts that there is at least some duty under section 150 (see section 7, Legal Framework at 7.2.3). At the time of writing no reported case on this point has come to the author's attention.

CHAPTER 8

Nuisance

Nuisance

Definition

"Nuisance may be defined...as any wrongful act or omission upon or near a highway, whereby the public are prevented from freely, safely, and conveniently passing along the highway."[43]

Nuisance is in fact any activity which materially affects the "reasonable comfort and convenience of life of a class of Her Majesty's subjects",[44] but we are mainly concerned here with the particular rules of nuisance affecting highways.

Because private nuisance concerns an interference with use and enjoyment of real property, we are concerned only with public nuisance. In highway slip and trip cases we usually find two instances of public nuisance relevant:

- nuisance arising by the defendant causing or permitting an obstruction;

- nuisance arising from an act or omission which makes the highway dangerous.

Cause of Action

A cause of action will only exist where a claimant can show that due to a defendant's action:

- there is a class of persons which has suffered damage

- s/he is one of that class

- some further, individual damage has been caused the claimant.

---

43 *Jacobs* v L.C.C. [1950] A.C. 361.
44 *A–G* v *PYA Quarries* [1957] 2 QB 169 at 184.

The individual claimant must show "some particular, direct and substantial loss or damage beyond that what is suffered by him in common with all other members of the public [injured]".[45] Showing mere inconvenience in common with others would not be enough to ground an action in public nuisance, but obviously in a trip and slip scenario this rule will not cause a difficulty.

Liability for Nuisance

The highway authority, or the tortfeasor of the nuisance where there is no one liable for the repair of the highway, will:

- be liable in damages
- for injuries which foreseeably result from that nuisance if
- it knew or ought to have know of the nuisance and
- failed to abate it

Public nuisance on highways usually takes one of three forms:

- interference with rights of access to/egress from property adjoining a highway

- damage caused by dangerous premises on the highway

- damage resulting from obstructions on the highway

The first is rarely of interest in trip and slip cases, but both the others often ground actions. The personal injury suffered as a result of such hazard or obstruction must be suffered on the highway and not on the premises abutting or adjoining the highway.[46] The injury suffered must be of a kind which was foreseeable. This is tantamount (in personal injury matters) to saying that fault is required. Although, strictly, it is not necessary to prove fault to succeed in public negligence, because "fault generally involves foreseeabilty"[47] then it in practice must be established. This causes little hardship for trip and slip claimants as it is difficult to envisage a scenario in which it would not be forseeable that an injury, actually suffered, might have been. Obstructions may be minute, yet important, in trip and slip lititagtion. An example of this is

---

45 *Harper v Haden & Sons* [1933] Ch 298.
46 *Bromley v Mercer* [1922] 2 KB 126.
47 *The Wagon Mound (No 2)* [1967] 1 AC 617.

found in *Dollman* v *Hillman Ltd*,[48] where fat flying from a butcher's premises and landing on the pavement grounded a successful action. Where an obstruction is caused by a natural hazard there is still a duty on the owner of the premises to deal with the nuisance, but has a reasonable time within which to so do.

Abatement

There is a common law duty to abate nuisance. Additionally, a local authority has a duty under section 130(3) and (4) of the Highways Act 1980:

> "....it is the duty of a council who are a highway authority to prevent, as far as possible, the stopping up or obstruction of –
>
> (a) the highway for which they are the highway authority, and
>
> (b) any highway for which they are not the highway authority, if, in their opinion, the stopping up or obstruction of that highway would be prejudicial to the interests of their area.
>
> (4) Without prejudice to the foregoing provisions of this section, it is the duty of a local highway authority to prevent any unlawful encroachment on any roadside waste comprised in a highway for which they are the highway authority.

Negligence or Nuisance?

Following on from abatement, the question may be asked "could winter maintenance cases be brought in nuisance?" Actions resulting from highway authorities' failure to clear snow and ice seem to have been brought exclusively under section 41 – the main "duty to maintain" provision – of the Highways Act 1980, before *Goodes*. As *Goodes* has established that there is no duty under section 41 to clear snow and ice we may see some claimants seeking to argue that accumulations of snow and ice on a highway are obstructions which constitute a nuisance. If the highway authority fails to remove such, the argument may be made, then it is arguably liable under section 130

---

48 *Dollman* v *Hillman Ltd* [1941] 1 All ER 355.

above. (Note the case of *Slater* v *Worthington's Cash Stores*[49] where the owners of a property were liable in public nuisance for an accumulation of snow which fell from their premises onto a claimant on the highway. What if the claimant had slipped on the accumulation instead?)

However it is worth noting at this stage that users of a highway have to assume some risk, which may on occasion amount to danger.

> "Traffic on the highways....cannot be conducted without exposing those whose persons or property are near to it to some inevitable risk, and ...those who go on the highway or have their property adjacent to it, may well be held to do so subject to their taking on themselves the risk of injury ..."

– this is as much the case today as when first uttered in *Rylands* v *Fletcher*.[50]

Temporary interference is allowable – it has to be, after all, to ensure we enjoy the benefits of public lighting, telephones, cable services and so forth.

Most actions in nuisance can be equally well founded on negligence, and indeed should be, at least in the alternative, unless – as in our instance of a highway for which there is no person liable to maintain – there is no breach of duty.

49 *Slater* v *Worthington's Cash Stores (1930) Ltd* [1941] 1 KB 488.
50 *Rylands* v *Fletcher* (1866) L.R. 1 Ex. 265.

SECTION 3
Premises

CHAPTER 9

Occupiers' Liability – Common Law and Statutory Duty

Occupiers' Liability – Common Law and Statutory Duty

Common Law Duty of Care

The common law duty of duty of care, owed by the occupiers of property to those on their premises, imposed varying standards of care dependant upon the class of visitor – whether the visitor was an invitee or licensee, entering under a contract and so forth.

Occupiers' Liability Act 1957

The Occupiers' Liability Act 1957 provided new rules – its main effect was to create a **"common duty of care"**. This replaced the old rules which differed according to the status of visitor. Occupiers' liability under the Act became more like liability in straightforward negligence. The common duty of care, defined in section 2(2) is a duty:

> to take such care as in all the circumstances of the case is reasonable to see that the visitor will be reasonably safe in using the premises for the purposes for which he is invited or permitted to be there.

The old common law duty of care is still here[51], but it coexists with the statutory common duty of care. However it seems:

> "there will be little, if any, practical difference between a plaintiff's remedy under the Act for breach of the common duty of care and his remedy at common law anyway. The issue in each case will be one of fact: has the duty to take reasonable care been broken?"[52]

---

51 See *Peskett v Portsmouth City Council* (2002) CA 25/6/2002, (Lawtel report) for an illustration.
52 *Clerk & Lindsell on Torts*, Ch 10 (18th ed) Sweet & Maxwell.

We are therefore going to focus on liability under the Occupiers Liability Act 1957 (and the Occupiers' Liability Act 1984 in relation to non-visitors).

What are premises?

It seems to be accepted that "land" would have been a better word to use than "premises"; there do not have to be buildings on the land for liability to accrue.

This is important in trip and slip cases – accidents on cleared sites, wasteland and even empty fields come within the definition of premises.

Section1(3)(a) of the Act provides that it also applies to the obligations of

> "a person occupying or having control over any fixed or movable structure, including any vessel, vehicle or aircraft".

Occupiers

Perhaps wisely, the Act provides no definition of "occupier". In *Wheat* v *E. Lacon*,[53] which turned on the meaning of "occupier" Lord Denning focused on the question of the extent of control. His Lordship said that wherever a person has a sufficient degree of control over premises:

> that he ought to realise that any failure on his part to use care may result in injury to a person coming lawfully there, then he is an "occupier" and the person coming lawfully there is his "visitor"

His Lordship went on to say that:

> [i]n order to be an "occupier" it is not necessary for a person to have entire control over the premises. He need not have exclusive occupation. Suffice it that he has some degree of control. He may share the control with others. Two or more may be "occupiers". And whenever this happens, each is under a duty to use care towards persons coming lawfully on to the premises, dependant on his degree of control. If each fails in his duty, each is liable to a visitor who is injured in consequence of his failure, but each may have a claim to contribution from the other.

---

53 *Wheat* v *E. Lacon & Co. Ltd* [1966] A.C. 552 at 577–579.

Indices of Occupancy

From the foregoing, to be an "occupier", it seems the following are relevant:

- there must be a sufficient degree of control over the premises

- sufficiency of control amounts to an ability to ensure the safety of the premises

- sufficiency of control also amounts to an appreciation that failure to use care may result in injury to others

- control need not be exclusive

- control need not extend to the entirety of the premises

- there must be some degree of actual physical control of the premises.

CHAPTER 10
Common Duty of Care

Common Duty of Care

Section 2, mentioned in part above, of the 1957 Act provides:

(1) An occupier of premises owes the same duty, the "common duty of care", to all his visitors, except in so far as he is free to and does extend, restrict, modify or exclude his duty to any visitor or visitors by agreement or otherwise.

(2) The common duty of care is a duty to take such care as in all the circumstances of the case is reasonable to see that the visitor will be reasonably safe in using the premises for the purposes for which he is invited or permitted by the occupier to be there.

The most important aspect of this is that all persons lawfully on the premises, whatever their class of entry to the land, are to be treated the same. This changed the common law distinction between, for example, invitees, licensees and those entering lawfully in other manners, such as those exercising rights of way.

See *Beaton* v *Devon County Council*[54] for a Court of Appeal's consideration of the correct standard of care.

Visitor

The Act provides that the common duty of care **relates to the visitor.** In this regard see section 2(3):

"The circumstances relevant for the present purpose include the degree of care, and want of care, which would ordinarily be looked for in such a visitor, so that (for example) in proper cases –

(a) an occupier must be prepared for children to be less careful than adults; and

(b) an occupier must expect that a person, in the exercise of his calling, will appreciate and guard against any special risk ordinarily incident to it, so far as the occupier leaves him free to do so."

---

54 *Beaton* v *Devon County Council* (2002) CA 31/10/2002, Lawtel report.

Reasonableness

A court will consider all the circumstances when evaluating reasonableness, such as:

- the purpose of the visit
- whether child or adult visitor
- occupiers' knowledge
- lighting
- warnings
- difficulty of removing the danger
- expense of removing the danger

Application

The best way of grasping the effect of the 1957 Act in the context of trip and slip is to look at how it has been applied in indicative cases.

For example, in *Adams v S.J. Watson & Co.*[55] a cleaner who slipped on a floor which had been polished to the degree that it had become dangerous succeeded in a personal injury action.

In *Jennings v British Railways Board*[56] litter was left strewn around a railway parcels office. A visitor who tripped over some of this litter succeeded against BR.

In *Hopkins v Scunthorpe Corporation*[57] failure to mop up melted snow in the entrance hall of a municipal library led to a plaintiff succeeding in an action against a local authority.

In *Murphy v City of Bradford*[58] the claimant slipped and fell on a sloping path after a snow fall. The path had been cleared and gritted, but the court held the cause of the fall was self-evidently the slipperiness of the path. A handrail was subsequently provided and the court held that its installation was an indication that the sloping pathway had been a candidate for special treatment.

On the other hand, in *Irving v L.C.C.*[59] a slip on an unlighted flight of steps in a block of flats went uncompensated, although the lack of

---

55 *Adams v S.J. Watson & Co.* (1967) 117 New L.J. 130.
56 *Jenning v British Railways Board* (1984) 134 New L.J. 584.
57 *Hopkins v Scunthorpe Corporation* [1966] C.L.Y. 8112.
58 *Murphy v City of Bradford Metropolitan Council* [1992] P.I.Q.R. P68 (CA).
59 *Irving v L.C.C.* (1965) 109 S.J. 157.

lighting was due to a time switches' faulty operation (however, see *Lighting* below). Similarly, in *Shortall* v *Greater London Council*[60] a claimant who fell through an empty panel in a door failed to succeed.

---

60 *Shortall* v *Greater London Council* (1969) 210 E.G.25.

CHAPTER 11
Children; Rescuers; Workers; Retailers; Contractors

Children; Rescuers; Workers; Retailers; Contractors

Children and Occupiers

Adults are more careful than children. An occupier has a duty to take this into consideration and to act accordingly. Section 2(3) of the 1957 Act provides that an occupier must be prepared for children to be less careful than adults.

Precautions and warnings which would be sufficient for adults may not suffice for children.

In particular, an occupier must be aware of features on the land which may be attractions, enticements or allurements to children.

The position regarding children is very different from that of those who may be expected to be able to guard themselves against obvious dangers, such as workmen (see below). However, an occupier is not expected to do more than exercise the degree of care for a child's safety than that which the occupier could reasonably assume would be exercised by the child's parent. It is probably the case that the law, post 1957 Act, remains the same as stated in *Phipps* v *Rochester Corporation*[61] where the primary duty for small childrens' safety rested, *per* Devlin J., upon their parents' shoulders:

> It is their duty to see that such children are not allowed to wander about by themselves, or at least to satisfy themselves that the places to which they do allow their children to go unaccompanied are safe for them to go to. It would not be socially desirable if parents were, as a matter of course, able to shift the burden of looking after their children from their own shoulders to those who happen to have accessible bits of land.

---

61 *Phipps v Rochester Corporation* [1955] 1 Q.B. 450.

Rescue services

Although it was established in *Sibbald or Bermingham* v *Sher Bros*[62] that an occupier has no liability to a firefighter simply because the condition of the premises make firefighters' tasks more dangerous, in the absence of special or unusual danger, nevertheless if the fire has been started negligently (as is often the case) the occupier may be liable under the general law of negligence.[63] In practice, with lifting injuries, slip and trips make up the bulk of claims by firefighters.

However in *Simpson* v *A1 Dairies Farms Ltd*[64] it was held that where an occupier was actually present at the scene of a fire in which the water pumped by the firefighters had caused a hazard by concealing a drain which, if it had remained exposed, would not have been dangerous, then that occupier was under a duty created by section 2 of the Occupiers' Liability Act 1957 to warn the firefighters at the scene of the hazard.

In *Neame* v *Johnson*[65] [1993] an ambulanceman, carrying the defendant who was unconscious, knocked over a pile of books left against a wall on a landing. The ambulanceman then slipped on one of the books and fell. Even though the lighting was admittedly "dismal" the defendant prevailed in this action for negligence and breach of statutory duty under the Occupiers' Liability Act 1957, section 2. The Court of Appeal held it was impossible to say that the pile of books gave rise to a reasonably foreseeable risk of personal injury to the claimant, in the circumstances of the case.

Workers

An occupier may, by section 2(3)(b) of the 1957 Act, expect that:

> "a person, in the exercise of his calling, will appreciate and guard against any special risks ordinarily incident to it, so far as the occupier leaves him free to do so."

---

62 *Sibbald or Bermingham* v *Sher Bros*, 1980 S.L.T. 122.
63 *Ogwo* v *Taylor* [1988] 1 A.C. 431.
64 *Simpson* v *A1 Dairies Farms Ltd* (2001) CA 12/1/2001 Lawtel report.
65 *Neame* v *Johnson* [1993] P.I.Q.R. P100.

This means, for example, that steeple-jacks and roofers should be left to judge for themselves such matters as load-bearing capacity, footrests, handholds and the like.

In *Clare* v *Whittaker & Son Ltd*[66] an occupier was held not liable for failing to tell experienced workmen to use crawling-boards which had been provided for their protection.

Lord Denning MR said in *Roles* v *Nathan*[67] that

> "[w]hen a householder calls in a specialist to deal with a defective installation on his premises, he can reasonably expect the specialist to appreciate and guard against the dangers arising from the defect."

Note the risks must be **ordinarily incident** to the workers task – if, for example, a worker trips over litter on the way to climb a ladder the ordinary rules set out above will apply.

Retail premises

A person on retail premises for the purposes of shopping is a visitor.

The personal injury solicitor will often encounter causes of action involving slips and trips in shops. The most cited case involving such an incident is *Ward* v *Tesco Stores Ltd* [1976] 1 All ER 219 (CA).

Here, the claimant had slipped on some spilled yoghurt in a supermarket aisle (see the extracts below in the section on *res ipsa loquitur* for more detail).

In the evidence it was established that:

- the defendants brushed the floor about half a dozen times a day

- any staff noticing a spillage were to call for its removal staff were to remain by the spill to guard against any accident in the interim.

The Court of Appeal held:

- the defendants had had sufficient time to clear up the spill;

- as they had not cleared it up there had not been an adequate inspection process.

---

66 *Clare* v *Whittaker & Son Ltd* [1976] I.C.R. 1, QBD.
67 *Roles* v *Nathan* [1963] I W.L.R. 1117.

Accordingly, and applying the maxim of *res ipsa loquitur* the court held in the claimant's favour.

Commentary on the case has indicated that it is felt that the standard of the common duty of care in that case was put at too high a level. The effect of this decision is to provide that once the claimant has established that something is where it should not have been then the burden of proof (of disproving negligence) is effectively transferred to the defendant.

"Walked-in" water causes some problems. This is water which is deposited on an area of flooring inside the entrance by visitors coming in when it has been raining outside. In the 2002 case of *Laverton* v *Kiapasha t/a Takeaway Supreme*[68] the Court of Appeal held in favour of the defendant, saying that it was reasonable to expect customers to take care on a tiled floor which was likely to be wet, and that walked-in water was not an unusual danger.

Statutory Duties on Retail Premises

The principal statutory duties as to the safety of floors, stairs etc. in retail premises are to be found under s.16 of the Offices, Shops and Railway Premises Act 1963.

Independent Contractors

The common law position, laid down in *Thompson* v *Cremin*, was that an occupier was liable for the danger created by a contractor invited onto the land. Section 2(4)(b) of the 1957 Act was intended to give the occupier some protection:

> "where damage is caused to a visitor by a danger due to the faulty execution of any work of construction, maintenance or repair by an independent contractor employed by the occupier, the occupier is not to be treated without more as answerable for the danger if in all the circumstance he had acted reasonably in entrusting the work to an independent contractor and had taken such steps (if any) as he reasonably ought in order to satisfy himself that the contractor was competent and that the work had been properly done."

---

68 *Laverton* v *Kiapasha t/a Takeaway Supreme*, CA, unreported, 19 November 2002.

This protection is very important in the general personal injury field, but it is submitted that it is less so in trip and slip cases than in others. The section is designed to protect an occupier in situations where technical knowledge or skill which an ordinary occupier could not reasonably be expected to have are required. Trips and slips are more often caused by activities, which although perhaps occasioned by contractors, do not in themselves require any specialist knowledge. This is well illustrated by two cases – *Haseldine* v *Daw* [69] and *Woodward* v *Mayor of Hastings* [70] – which although they predate the Act, nevertheless give a good indication of the way in which the section we are concerned with is likely to be applied.

In *Haseldine* a lift failed having been negligently repaired by an occupier's contractors. It was held that the occupier's duty had been discharged by employing a competent firm of engineers to periodically inspect and adjust it. It was said the occupier:

> "does not profess as such to be....a hydraulic engineer. Having no technical skill he cannot rely on his own judgement, and the duty of care towards his invitees requires him to obtain and follow good technical advice. **If he did not** (*emphasis added*) do so, he would, indeed, be guilty of negligence."

In *Woodward* the claimant slipped on an icy step left in that condition by the negligence of a cleaner, an independent contractor. The court distinguished *Haseldine*, pointing out that no technical knowledge was required in cleaning the instant case:

> " ...there is no esoteric quality in the nature of the work which the cleaning of a snow-covered step demands."

This lack of technical knowledge will be relevant in many tripping and slipping scenarios.

An occupier must not do work involving such specialised knowledge and skill that a reasonable occupier would employ experts to do. In this context this usually means electrical work, boiler maintenance and lift repairs must be carried out by persons qualified and experienced in such work. An occupier may however carry out work such as carpentry, and will if engaged in such activity be held to the standard of a reasonably competent amateur.

---

69 *Haseldine* v *Daw* [1941] 2 K.B. 343.
70 *Woodward* v *Mayor of Hastings* [1954] K.B. 174.

In certain circumstances, there may be a duty to ensure that independent contractors are adequately covered by public liability insurance.[71]

Summary

An occupier must:

- take reasonable steps to ensure a contractor is competent;

- take reasonable steps to ensure the work has been done competently, if the nature of the work so permits.

Lighting

There is no proposition that an occupier is required to light all area in times of darkness. However if there is an invitation to use premises in the dark, the occupier has a duty of protection. This duty may be discharged by lighting, warning or otherwise.

As ever, examples from cases give the best guidance in any instance, as here, where there is no absolute rule. For instance:

- in *Hawkins* v *Coulsdon and Purley U.D.C*[72] the claimant recovered when she fell on a broken step in the dark while gaining access to a premises she had been invited to enter;

- in *Ghannan* v *Glasgow Corp.*[73] the injured party was held two-fifths to blame for walking about in the dark without a light;

- in *Neame* v *Johnson*[74] "dismal" lighting conditions did not affect a finding of the defendant's absence of negligence in leaving a pile of books on a landing.

---

71 *Gurilliam* v *West Hertfordshire Hospital NHS Trust & Ors.* [2002] EWCA Civ 1041.
72 *Hawkins* v *Coulsdon and Purley U.D.C* [1953] 1 W.L.R. 882.
73 *Ghannan* v *Glasgow Corp* 1950 S.C. 23.
74 *Neame* v *Johnson* [1993] P.I.Q.R. P100.

Trespassers; Rights of Way; Volenti; Warnings

Trespassers; Rights of Way; Volenti; Warnings

Trespassers

As trespassers are not visitors the Occupiers Liability Act 1957 has no application. Traditionally, trespassers were sternly dealt with by the common law. Lord Dunedin in *Robert Addie & Sons (Collieries) Ltd* v *Dumbreck*[75] defined a trespasser as a person who goes

> "on [to] the land without invitation of any sort and whose presence is either unknown to the proprietor or, if known, is practically objected to".

In that case Lord Hailsham said that

> "[t]owards the trespasser the occupier has no duty to take reasonable care for his protection or even to protect him from concealed danger.
>
> The trespasser comes on to the premises at his own risk. An occupier is in such cases liable only where the injury is due to some wilful act involving something more than the absence of reasonable care. There must be some act done with the deliberate intention of doing harm to the trespasser, or at least some act done with reckless disregard to the presence of the trespasser."

This was strong stuff. What about the situation where trespass was inadvertent, or where the trespasser was a child? After *Addie* v *Drumbreck* the courts became inventive in finding ways of ameliorating the harshness of the rule. Examples of artificial avoidance techniques included:

- implied licence where a landowner knew of regular trespass;

- the legal fiction of "allurement", where a landowner kept something attractive to children near the edge of his property.

---

75 *Robert Addie & Sons (Colieries) Ltd* v *Dumbreck* [1929] A.C. 358.

In any event in 1972 in *British Railways Board* v *Herrington*[76] the House of Lords reversed *Addie* – this reversal thought by many to indicate disapproval of the harshness of the regime. In *Herrington* British Rail had knowingly left a fence in bad repair next to a railway line; a child entered onto the line, which was electrified, and was burnt. The court held that a limited duty of care was in fact owed to trespassers.

After *Herrington* the situation was imprecise:

- what was the level of the duty owed to trespassers?
- how did it differ from the duty owed to lawful visitors?

In the years after *Herrington* the courts in practice came to treat actions brought by trespassers under ordinary negligence principles.

It was felt that the situation was imprecise. The Occupiers Liability Act 1984 was in due course enacted to codify the common law rules which had been applied post-*Herrington*.

Section 1(4) of the 1984 Act provides that an occupier has a duty to take such care "as is reasonable in all the circumstances of the case to see that the trespasser does not suffer injury on the premises", such injury being occasioned by a danger on the said premises. The duty is subject to the provisos that the occupier:

- knows, or ought to know, of the existence of danger on the land; and

- knows, or ought to know, that the trespasser is in the vicinity of the danger.

The duty is also subject to the provision in s.1(3) that the risk

"is one against which, in all the circumstances of the case, he may reasonably be expected to offer some protection".

---

76 *British Railways Board* v *Herrington* [1972] A.C. 877.

Standard of Care

"Reasonable expectation, in all the circumstances" – this is less than precise. Best practice in estimating the standard of care in a particular case may be to look for precedents in post-*Herrington* decisions, as the 1984 Act was designed to codify the body of law thus built up.

The standard will differ depending on the motives of the trespasser. A burglar who trips over items left on a landing and is injured by the subsequent fall down a flight of stairs is unlikely to be afforded the protection of the Act; a child who wanders into the same building if left unlocked and who suffers the same fate will in all likelihood be covered. *Clerk & Lindsell on Torts* has a useful list of examples of trespasser-claimant actions for personal injury.

Two factors are important when considering the standard:

- the seriousness of the danger
- the type of trespasser

The first is self-explanatory – in our context an occupier has a greater duty concerning premises which are slippery, or ill-lit, and which have machinery or dangerous substances into which a resulting fall would be very injurious.

The second mainly relates to the child trespasser. It is the case that an occupier must take greater care for the safety of children than for the safety of adults. In *Nwabudike* v *Southwark LBC*[77] (1996) it was noted that once a school has taken "all necessary and proper steps" in order to ensure the safety of its pupils it is not in breach of its duty of care when an accident happens "even though the standard of that duty is a high one". Active steps must be taken where it would be reasonable to anticipate the presence of child visitors – for example, in circumstances where it would be sufficient to erect a warning sign for adults, a fence may be required for children. In some instances, however, a warning sign may not be enough even for adults, if they have been shown to be ineffective in the past.[78]

---

77 *Nwabudike* v *Southwark LBC* (19660 *The Times*, 28 June.
78 *Tomlinson* v *Congleton Borough Council & Anor* (2002) [2002] EWCA Civ 309.

Retributive measures

There are a number of case on injuries caused by measures designed to keep trespassers out, but these are in the main ordinary – rather than trip and slip – personal injury cases and so do not need to be dealt with here. In circumstances where it is conceivable that, say, a tripping injury was caused by such a measure the court will concern itself with whether it was deterrent or retributive. Measures, obvious from outside the premises and intended *only* to deter, will be approved.[79] However, a pathway deliberately made greasy to deter prowlers, for example, would in all likelihood be classed as a hidden danger and a resulting slip would in such case be grounds for action.

Exclusion of Liability

Section 2(1) of the Unfair Contract Terms Act 1977 provides that a business cannot exclude liability for personal injury caused by negligence, or under the Occupiers' Liability Act 1957. The section says, in part:

> [a] person cannot by reference to any contract term or to a notice given to persons generally or to particular persons exclude or restrict his liability for death or personal injury.

It would appear however that it is at least arguable that liability under the 1984 Act (in which the 1977 Act is not mentioned) may lawfully be excluded, which is an anomaly and almost certainly not one intended by the framers of the legislation.

Rights of Way

The occupier of land over which a public right of way passes is not liable as an occupier for any accident which occurs on that right of way. They are not invitees of the occupier nor are they visitors under the 1957 Act.

In *McGeown v Northern Ireland Housing Executive*[80] the question whether an owner of land over which there was a right of way was

---

79 *Cummings v Grainger* [1977] Q.B..
80 *McGeown v Northern Ireland Housing Executive* 3 WLR 187.

liable for negligent nonfeasance towards members of the public received close scrutiny. In that case the claimant was the tenant of the defendant on a housing estate, which was surrounded by open land which formed part of the estate. There were a number of footpaths over which the public had right of way. The claimant tripped in a hole in one of the paths and fell, breaking her leg. The claimant did not succeed in her court of first instance, nor before the Court of Appeal for Northern Ireland, and the matter in due course came before the House of Lords who were, in summary, asked to decide:

- that the rule (known as the rule in *Gautret* v *Egerton*[81]) that owners of land over which a public right of way passed were not liable for negligent nonfeasance was no longer good law;

- that the claimant appellant was not only a member of the public but also a visitor owed a duty by the landowner under the Northern Irish equivalent of section 2 of the 1957 Act.

The claimant did not succeed. The court held that the rule that the owner of land over which there passed a public right of way was under no liability for negligent nonfeasance was indeed good law. It would be unreasonable if landowners, who had to allow the passage over the land of any person who wished to do so, also had a duty to maintain that land in a safe condition. The rule in *Gautret* v *Egerton* was upheld (see also *Holden* v *White*[82]; *Greenhalgh* v *British Railways Board*[83]) and the observation of Willes J. in that case was quoted approvingly by Lord Keith of Kinkel:

> "It may be the duty of the defendants to abstain from doing any act which may be dangerous to persons coming upon the land by their invitation or permission...But, what duty does the law impose upon these defendants to keep their [land] in repair? If I dedicate a way to the public which is full of ruts and holes, the public must take it as it is. If I dig a pit in it, I may be liable for the consequences: but, if I do nothing, I am not."

---

81 *Gautret* v *Egerton* (1867) LR 2 CP 371.
82 *Holden* v *White* [1982] QB 679.
83 *Greenhalgh* v *British Railways Board* [1969] 2 QB 286.

Lord Keith went on to note that Lord Denning MR also selected this observation for approval in *Greenhalgh* and continued

> "[Greenhalgh and Holden] are sufficient to show that the rule in Gautret v. Egerton is deeply entrenched in the law. Further, the rule is in my opinion undoubtedly a sound and reasonable one. Rights of way pass over many different types of terrain, and it would place an impossible burden upon landowners if they not only had to submit to the passage over them of anyone who might choose to exercise them but also were under a duty to maintain them in a safe condition. Persons using rights of way do so not with the permission of the owner of the solum but in the exercise of a right. There is no room for the view that such persons might have been licensees or invitees of the landowner under the old law or that they are his visitors under the British or Northern Irish Acts of 1957."

Therefore, the court said, the claimant could not claim either under the 1957 Act or at common law.

Volenti non fit injuria

Section 2(5) of the 1957 Act provides:

> The common duty of care does not impose on an occupier any obligation to a visitor in respect of risks willingly accepted as his by the visitor (the question whether a risk was so accepted to be decided on the same principles as in other cases in which one person owes a duty of care to another).

Volenti has always been a defence available to an occupier at common law, and the situation has not been changed by the 1957 Act. However:

- the danger must be willingly accepted
- this involves appreciating the exact risk in advance[84]
- the injury must be due solely to the fault of the injured party.[85]

---

84 See *White v Blackmore* [1972] 2 Q.B. 651 in relation to the difference between participating in dangerous sports, and the dangers of spectating at dangerous sports.
85 See *Slater v Clay Cross Co. Ltd* [1956] 2 Q.B. 264 per Denning L.J. at 271.

Warnings and Exclusion of Liability

Under the common law a warning, provided the visitor could be shown to have appreciated the full significance of the risk, was sufficient to excuse the occupier from liability.[86] The situation has been changed by the 1957 Act which in section 2(4) provides:

> "In determining whether the occupier of premises has discharged the common duty of care to a visitor, regard is to be had to all the circumstances, so that (for example)–
>
> (a) where damage is caused to a visitor by a danger of which he had been warned by the occupier, the warning is not to be treated without more as absolving the occupier from liability, unless in all the circumstances it was enough to enable the visitor to be reasonably safe."

This means that an understood warning does not preclude recovery – it is merely one of the matters to be taken into consideration. The court will consider:

- how serious was the danger
- how specific was the warning[87]
- where the warning was placed (e.g. too high, too distant)
- the tone and import of the warning (e.g. oral warnings given casually[88] may not suffice)
- was the warning sufficient to enable the visitor to be reasonably safe.

Only if the court is satisfied on these points will the occupier be held to have satisfied the duty of care.

---

86 *London Graving Dock v Horton* [1951] A.C. 737.
87 See *Rae v Mars (U.K.) Ltd* (1989) *The Times*, February 15.
88 *Bishop v J.S.Starnes & Sons* [1971] 1 Lloyd's Rep. 162.

CHAPTER 13
Landlords

Landlords

To let a property is to part with all physical control.[89] A landlord is not an occupier under the Act. Note the following however:

- a landlord has duties under sections 3 and 4 of the Defective Premises Act 1972

- a landlord has common law duties

- a landlord is occupier of any areas not demised (such as common stairways, hall and such).

At common law a landlord is liable for defects caused by the landlord's negligence; this is so whether the defects predate the lease or not.

However, if a landlord is a licensor rather than an lessor then that landlord may be liable even for defects not negligently caused (see *Graham v N.I. Housing Executive*[90] where a housing authority was liable to a squatter who was also a licensee).

Defective Premises Act 1972

Section 3 of the Defective Premises Act 1972, section 3 provides:

> (1) Where work of construction, repair, maintenance or demolition or any other work is done on or in relation to premises, any duty of care owed, because of doing the work, to persons who might reasonably be expected to be affected by defects in the state of the premises created by the doing of the work shall not be abated by the subsequent disposal of the premises by the persons who owed the duty.

Section 4 deals with defects which arise during the term of a lease. If defects arise in a premises this section imposes a statutory duty of care if:

- the landlord has a duty to repair under the lease; or

---

89 *Wheat v E. Lacon & Co. Ltd* [1966] A.C. 552.
90 *Graham v N.I. Housing Executive* (1986) 8 N.I.JB. 93.

- the landlord has a right of entry to repair or maintain.

This statutory duty

- is not dependant on notice of a defect[91];

- is owed to all persons "who might reasonably be expected to be affected by defects in the premises";

- is also owed to those who might be foreseeably affected while on the premises (this includes trespassers);

- is a duty to take such care "as is reasonable in the circumstances";

- the extent of the duty to take care is to see that those likely to be affected by a defect are reasonably safe.

What of the situation where there is no obligation on the landlord under the lease to repair or maintain? Well, obviously there may, in some circumstances, be a case in contract as between the landlord and the tenant grounded on implied terms. In addition, there is the Landlord and Tenant Act 1985 and the situation at common law to consider.

Landlord and Tenant Act 1985

Section 11(1) provides that an obligation to keep the structure and exterior of a dwellinghouse in repair shall be implied into any lease of less than seven years (other than new leases to existing tenants). The installations for the supply of gas, water and electricity, and for sanitation, are also covered by this section. Section 116 of the Housing Act 1988 extends this section to encompass certain parts of the building and installations outside the demised premises.

Prior to 15 January 1989 (the date on which section 116 of the 1988 Act came into effect) the exterior and structure to which section 11 of the 1985 Act related was the "structure and exterior of the flat itself" – see *Campden Hill Towers* v *Gardner*[92] – and not the block it was in. Under any lease made subsequent to that date (unless made pursuant to a contract made before Jan 15 1989) the landlord's obligation

---

91 *Sykes* v *Harry & Anor* [2001] EWCA Civ 167.
92 *Campden Hill Towers* v *Gardner* [1977] QB 823.

extends to any part of the building in which the landlord has an interest or estate.

The duty under section 11 of the 1985 Act is more onerous that that created by section 4 of the Defective Premises Act. Under section 4 there is a duty to take such care as is reasonable in the circumstances to see that persons who might reasonably be expected to be affected by defects in the premises are safe. Under s.11 however there is an absolute duty to keep in repair the structure and exterior.

Notice

Before section 11 will operate so as to imply a covenant against a landlord notice of the defects to be remedied must be given.

Privity

Section 11 implies a covenant into the lease, and therefore any action grounded on a breach of that covenant will be a claim in contract. By definition therefore section 11 will only be relevant in trip and slip litigation when the claimant is the tenant.

Landlord's Defence

There is no statutory defence to section 11 as originally drafted. However, the extension inserted by section 116 of the Housing Act 1988 applies to areas of the premises which, while forming part of the landlord's estate or interest, may not be parts to which access may be obtained to carry out works or repairs. If a landlord can prove that despite using all reasonable endeavours he was unable to obtain such rights as would enable him to carry out the necessary repairs then section 116 of the 1988 act inserts that fact as a statutory defence in section 11(3A) of 1985 Act.

Common Law

The general principle is that

- there is no duty on the landlord to put premises into repair[93] at the commencement of a tenancy

- there is no duty on the landlord to keep in repair or carry out repairs during the tenancy

absent the lease (or legislation) specifying otherwise.

However, in *Liverpool City Council* v *Irwin*[94] the House of Lords held there was an obligation to maintain common lifts, stairs and rubbish chutes in a high rise building. From a trip and slip perspective, this case is important since it held that there was a duty to provide adequate lighting, natural light being insufficient in these areas. It may be – and so appears from some later cases – that *Irwin* applies only in instances where access to the premises remains in the control of the landlord, but it nevertheless is a departure from the common law principle that once a landlord has parted with control of the premises he has parted with liability for defects.

It is worth emphasising that there is no common law immunity for defects which have been created by a landlord's own negligence, whether such took place before or after the lease was entered into.

---

93 But note in *Collins* v *Hopkins* [1923] 2 K.B. 617 it was held that there is an implied warranty in the letting of furnished premises that they are fit for human habitation at the commencement of the tenancy.

94 *Liverpool City Council* v *Irwin* [1977] AC 239.

SECTION 4
Slips and Trips at work

CHAPTER 14
Trips and Slips at work – Basic Principles

Trips and Slips at work – Basic Principles

General Points

Historically, slips and trips have been the most important cause of serious injuries at work. The HSE reported that in 1993/4 the most common cause (36%) of non-fatal major injuries to employees was a slip, trip or fall. The percentage of slip, trip or fall as a proportion of all major injuries rose steadily from 26% in 1986/7 to 36% in 1993/4. To take one year as an example, slips and trips in 1993/4 were estimated to have cost employers £300 million per year; in that 12-month period over 33,000 slip, trip and fall injuries were reported. Since then there has been no indication that matters have improved.

Severity of Injury

Again, historical statistics show the importance of this area to the slip and trip litigator. For example, slips, trips and falls on the same level experienced by employees resulted in an average of three deaths per year[95] in the period 1991/1992 to 1995/1996. Over that time approximately 5,700 non-fatal major injuries were suffered each year[96] from the same cause; between 25,000 and 30,000 injuries per annum[97] resulting in an absence from work of over 3 days were recorded. No figures are available for more minor slips and trips at work but it is thought that the figure is considerably in excess of 50,000 per year.

---

95 Government Statistical Service *Health and Safety Statistics* 1995/1996 HMSO (1996). See also *Health and Safety at Work: A Modern Guide* (2002) EMIS Professional Publishing.
96 Ibid.
97 Ibid.

EU Directives

This area of personal injury practice was revolutionised as a result of the implementation of European Directives on health and safety at work.

A difference in approach between the regulations which have come into force pursuant to Directives and the pre-existing domestic legislation is that the new regulations look to the type of **risk** – in our case, slips and trips – rather than to the type of **premises**.

Basic Principles

As said in *Donoghue* v *Stephenson*:[98]

> "the cardinal principle is that the party complained of should owe to the party complaining a duty to take care, and that the party complaining shall be able to prove that he has suffered damage in consequence of a breach of that duty."

The duty in question has been imposed upon employers either as a result of the general principles of negligence or as a consequence of statute.

A claimant employee in a tripping and slipping case must establish:

- the duty of care owed
- a breach of that duty
- injury resulting from that breach.

Duty of Care

An employer has a duty

> "to take personal care of the safety of his workmen, whether the employers can be an individual, a firm, or a company, and whether or not the employer takes any share in the conduct of the operation".[99]

The employer's duty is:

- personal
- non-delegable

---

98 *Donoghue* v *Stephenson* [1932] AC 562.
99 *Wilson's and Clyde Coal Co Ltd* v *English* [1938] AC 57.

- continuing.

However it is not absolute. An employer is allowed weigh up the cost of providing all possible safeguards against the risks to employees. As an example, in *Latimer* v *AEC Ltd*[1] the defendants had to measure the cost of closing down a factory against the risk of their employees slipping on oil spilled on a floor. The House of Lords held in this case that it had not been proved a "reasonably prudent" employer would have closed the factory, remedial measures not being possible.

Special Vulnerability

If an employee has a special vulnerability and that is not known to the employer, and there is no reason that the employer ought to have known of it, then there is no higher or extra duty owed. However, the duty is owed to each employee as an individual. Therefore, if an employee has a particular characteristic which makes him/her more likely to slip or trip, or to be more seriously injured in the event of such an accident, *and the employer knows of it or ought reasonably to have known of it,* then the employer has a duty to take that peculiar vulnerability into account.[2]

Employers' Warnings

If there is a risk of slipping or tripping which is not obvious, and which cannot be guarded against, an employer has a duty to warn any prospective employee of such.

Standard of Duty of Care

Assuming that a duty of care is established in a particular situation, the next question is what the standard of that care should be.

At common law negligence may be evidenced by both acts or omissions. With tripping and slipping accidents the first place we look to establish the standard of care is the general and approved practice in

---

1   *Latimer v AEC Ltd* [1953] AC 643.
2   *McDermid v Nash Dredging and Reclamation Co Ltd* [1987] AC 906.

industry. However, that it was general and approved practice will not excuse an activity which was clearly unsafe – for example, to wash down restaurant kitchen floors with soapy water may be general practice but unless the floor is then rinsed and mopped the standard of care will not be reached.

Forseeability

The damage resulting from the breach of care must have sufficient connection with the negligent act or omission so as to have been foreseeable. There is a chain of causation, which all lawyers will know from *The Wagon Mound (No 1)*:[3]

- Defendant must have been negligent
- Claimant's damage must have been caused by the negligence
- Damage must have been foreseeable

Extent of Damage

The *"damage may be a good deal greater in extent than was foreseeable. [A plaintiff] can only escape liability if the damage can be regarded as differing in kind from that what was foreseeable…"*.[4]

Therefore, if a tripping accident results in catastrophic injury – say due to an unusually weak spine – a negligent defendant will be liable unless such injury can be shown to differ in foreseeable **kind** and not in foreseeable **extent**. Liability for the full extent of the injury – the eggshell skull principle – is well established in circumstances where a defendant has been negligent.

Material Contribution

In some cases the defendant's negligent act or omission will not have been the entire cause of the claimant's injury. Indeed it may not have even been the principal cause of the damage. However, in such

---

3   *Overseas Tank Ship (UK) Ltd v Morts Dock and Engineering Co Ltd, The Wagon Mound* [1961] AC 388.
4   *Hughes v Lord Advocate* [1963] AC 837.

instances a claimant will prevail if it can be shown that the defendant's act or omission made a material contribution to the injury.

What is a material contribution? Virtually any contribution which does not come within the exception of *de minimis non curat lex* will be material. Thereafter it will be a question for the court to determine the degree of contribution.

Burden of Proof

In tripping and slipping negligence cases, as in any other personal injury action, the claimant has to establish the elements of the tort. The burden is very clearly on the claimant who will not succeed unless the court is satisfied that the accident was caused by the negligence of the other party. This is well illustrated in *Dixon* v *London Fire and Civil Defence Authority*.[5] In that case an employee had slipped and injured himself on the floor of a fire station. The floor, which was tiled, had been wet by water leaking from an appliance. It was accepted that water on floors was to be found, and expected, in fire stations. The problem of leaks in that working environment was endemic and insoluble. The court found that to discharge his burden the claimant would have to show that the fire authority had failed to take any reasonable steps to cure the problem. The court held that the claimant failed to so show, and that as a result he could not succeed in his action.

The burden will be discharged on the basis of the balance of probability.

---

5   *Dixon* v *London Fire and Civil Defence Authority* (1993) *The Times*, 22 February.

CHAPTER 15

Statutory Duty

Statutory Duty

Health and Safety at Work etc Act 1974

The Robens Committee on Safety and Health at Work 1970–1972 recommended that one single piece of legislation be introduced to provided a coherent system of health and safety legislation. This was to replace the existing very considerable body of primary and subordinate legislation then in existence – the Factories Act 1961, the Offices, Shops and Railway Premises Act 1963, the Mines and Quarries Act 1954, the Agriculture (Safety, Health and Welfare Provisions) Act 1956 and so forth – amounting in all to approximately 30 statutes and 500 sets of regulations.

As a result of the Robens Committee's report the Health and Safety at Work etc Act 1974 (H&SAWA) was implemented. Departing from the traditional practice of focusing on particular workplaces or types of work, the Act stated safety objectives in general terms. An onus was placed on employers to construct a safety policy. The general duties imposed by the H&SAWA do not in themselves give rise to civil liability, being too broad to be useful in that capacity, but the Act provided that the existing statutory provisions should be replaced with regulations and Approved Codes of Practice (ACOPs) which do impose such liability (unless provided otherwise).

It should be noted that many of existing statutory provisions have not been replaced. These remain in force. However, the general duties imposed by the H&SAWA **apply in addition** to those imposed by the earlier legislation.

Duty

Section 2(1) imposes a duty on:

> "every employer to ensure, as far as is reasonably practicable, the health, safety and welfare of all of his employees".

This means, in the context of trip and slip, that an employer must ensure:

- a safe system of work
- a safe place of work
- safe plant and machinery
- proper training
- proper supervision
- proper storage of substances
- proper transport of substances

remembering always that the Act does not provide for civil liability, but for HSE enforcement and criminal sanctions.

As far as civil liability is concerned, what the Act does do is lay a foundation, in section 15 and section 82, for health and safety regulations (the "six-pack"), which do, except where otherwise specifically provided, impose civil liability.

The Regulations

What do these regulations do, from the perspective of trip and slip lawyers?

Firstly, there is an emphasis on accident prevention. This is seen in particular in a requirement to *assess risk*, and act upon the assessment by taking steps to remove or minimise identified dangers.

Secondly, there are new duties imposed on **employees** in addition to the obligations provided for in the 1974 Act. These are:

- to use plant and equipment in accordance with instructions or training;

- to inform the employer of serious or imminent danger;

- to inform the employer of shortcomings in protective arrangements;

- to make use of personal protective equipment in accordance with instructions or training;

- to report any defect in or loss of personal protective equipment;
- to make full use of manual load handling systems.

CHAPTER 16

Management of Health and Safety at Work Regulations 1999

Management of Health and Safety at Work Regulations 1999

Framework Directive

These regulations have been implemented as of 29 December 1999 under the Framework Directive – Council Directive 89/391/EEC, otherwise cited as the *COUNCIL DIRECTIVE OF 12 JUNE 1989 on the introduction of measures to encourage improvements in the safety and health of workers* – and replace the 1992 regulations of the same name. These regulations – known as the Head Regulations, and sometimes referred to as the "Management" Regulations – did not require new implementing legislation – they were made under s.15 of the H&SAWA. The Head Regulations are very wide in scope. They have as their focus an obligation on all employers (and the self-employed) to carry out a risk assessment. Regulation 3 provides that assessment must be "suitable and sufficient" and address:

- the risks to the health and safety of [the] employees to which they are exposed whilst they are at work;

- the risks to the health and safety of persons not in his employment arising out of or in connection with the conduct by him of his undertaking.

Note that Reg 3 of the 1999 Regulations no longer requires a record of the risk assessment to be kept. This is a change from the 1992 Regulations. However, see Reg 5(2) in relation to a requirement to keep records for employers employing five or more persons.

There are five subsidiary sets of regulations (the Subsidiary Regulations); the Head and Subsidiary regulations together are known colloquially as the "six-pack". Those containing provisions particularly relevant to tripping and slipping cases[6] are:

- Workplace (Health, Safety and Welfare) Regulations 1992 (Workplace Regs)

- Provision and Use of Work Equipment Regulations 1998 (PUWER)

- Personal Protective Equipment at Work Regulations 1992 (PPE Regs)

- Manual Handling Operations Regulations 1992 (Manual Handling Regs).

ACOPs

The Regulations are supplemented by Approved Codes of Practice (ACOPs) and Guidance Notes. ACOPs and guidance notes are used to supplement the regulations. They cover much ground and it has been suggested that in personal injury practice the ACOPs/guidance notes may come to be more important than the regulations they refer to. For example the WHSW ACOP goes into very considerable detail on the standards which the regulations actually require, the Manual Handling Regulations have useful diagrams and all the ACOPs/Guidance Notes carry within them a short version of the text of the regulations which they then deal with in some depth.

Implementation

The Head Regulations and the Regulations came into effect on January 1, 1993. However, the subsidiary Regulations came into force on January 1, 1996 for workplaces used as such for the first time (or modified, extended or converted) after December 31, 1992.

---

6   The only one of the six-pack not directly relevant to trips and slips is the *Health and Safety (Display Screen Equipment) Regulations 1992* (VDU Regs).

Liability

The Health and Safety at Work Act 1974 provides under section 47(2) that

> Breach of duty imposed by health and safety Regulations shall, so far as it causes damage, be actionable except in so far as the Regulations provide otherwise.

However, the Head Regulations DO provide otherwise, unfortunately.

From a slip and trip lawyers perspective, the immediate problem is that the Head Regulations provide in reg. 22 under the heading **Exclusion of Civil Liability** that:

> Breach of a duty imposed by these Regulations shall not confer a right of action in any civil proceedings.

This is a bald statement, unadorned even by any expansion or justification in the accompanying Approved Code of Practice. (Note that there is no such exclusion in the five subsidiary sets of Regulations; breach of any of these can accordingly by relied upon as the basis for an action for breach of statutory duty.) There are two exceptions, which relate to:

1) the protection provided to new or expectant mothers by reg.16(1);

2) the protection provided to young persons by reg.19.

So why are we dealing with the Head Regulations at all in a personal injury practice text?

Firstly, we are doing so for the very good reason that while there may be no **direct** civil liability there may be **indirect** liability sufficient to support a common law negligence action. Although reg. 22 excludes a right of action, this does not mean that the regulations cannot be relied upon as providing **evidence** of required standards or steps to be taken by an employer; it may be that failure to comply with the regulations is evidence in itself of negligence.

Secondly, we need to be aware that by excluding civil liability there is an argument that the Head Regulations have failed to fully implement the Framework Directive. Under the Directive there is a requirement to provide full and adequate remedies. In *Von Colson and Kamann* v *Land Nordrhein-Westfalen*[7] it was noted that Member

---

7   *Von Colson and Kamann* v *Land Nordrhein-Westfalen*: 14/83 [1984] ECR 1891 ECJ.

States must make rights established by EU legislation a reality. This principle would allow the Commission only, and not private individuals, to take up any failure to implement, with the UK government. It is also now accepted that **individuals** also may have directly enforceable rights under Directives.[8] As the Head Regulations provide for criminal and administrative penalties only, there is a obviously then an argument that a Community right is not one which is a reality, absent any civil liability for breach. It is accepted that where there is any conflict between EU law and domestic law, then EU law will prevail, in most cases, and be enforced by domestic courts. The Treaty of Rome states that a Directive is binding as to the **result** to be achieved [by the member states] but "shall leave to the national authorities choice of form and methods".

The regulations are the "form and methods". The language of the regulations will naturally differ from the Directive. What is the situation then if there is any question of interpretation? In *Litster v Forth Dry Dock and Engineering Co Ltd* [1989] IRLR 161 the concept of "purposive construction" was devised:

> If the legislation can reasonably be construed so as to conform with those obligations....such a purposive construction will be applied even though, perhaps, it may involve some departure from the strict and literal application of the words which the legislature has elected to use.

However it appears that even if they adopt a purposive approach courts will not be willing to **strike out** words from the regulations even if they do not comply with Directive obligations as a result. Accordingly reg. 15 will stand under *Litster*. What else remains? Fortunately for a claimant personal injury lawyer we have the decision in *Francovich*,[9] followed up by *Brasserie*[10] and *British Telecommunications*.[11]

In *Francovich* it was established that where an individual has suffered loss or damage as a result of a member state's failure to implement a Directive then there is a right to compensation under EU law, which claim should be brought in a domestic court.

---

8   *Van Duyn v Home Office*: 41/74 [1975] Ch 358, ECJ; *Marshall v Southampton and South West Hampshire Area Health Authority (Teaching)*: 152/84 [1986] IRLR 140.

9   *Francovich v Italian Republic* [1992] IRLR 84.

10 Cases C–46/93 & C–48/93 *Brasserie du Pecheur & Factortame III* [1996] 1 CMLR 889.

11 Case C–392/93 *R v HM Treasury*, ex parte British Telecommunications [1996] 2 CMLR 217.

If

the Directive conferred rights for the benefit of the individual, those rights might be determined by reference to the Directive

and

there is a causal link between the states breach of obligation and the damage suffered by the individual

then

the member state may be liable for damages.

There is no doubt that the Framework Directive did confer rights on individuals, which rights are capable of determination by reference to the Directive, and it is not difficult to imagine a scenario wherein there might be a causal link between damage suffered by an individual and the breach by a member state.

To take the question of enforcement of the Framework Directive further is outside the scope of this text. It is sufficient to have outlined the rationale for the argument that even the Head Regulations may have application in civil liability. Litigators are referred to *Health and Safety: A Modern Guide*[12] for a straightforward further development of this aspect of the regulations.

It is also worth noting here that the Health and Safety Commission when drafting the Head Regulations took the view that some of the Directive's requirements were already met by existing legislation. An often cited example of this is that the duties placed on employers under Article 6 of the Directive are already required by the *Health and Safety at Work Act 1974*, section 2. However, the duties in the 1974 Act are very general when compared to the quite specific duties required by Article 6. The question is not whether the Head Regulations impose duties more or less specific than those already required by existing regulations, but whether existing regulations and the Head Regulations together suffice to comply with the Directive. At least as far as Art. 6 is concerned the answer to that question must be in the negative. (As a further example the apparent willingness of the drafters of the Head Regulations not to fully comply with the Directive we might here also take note that the Regulations provide for exemptions where five or

---

12 *Health and Safety: A Modern Guide*, Zindani, EMIS Professional Publishing 2002.

fewer persons are employed. The Directive makes no provisions for such an exemption.)

Subsidiary regulations; Civil liability

From the point of view of the personal injury lawyer an action supported by an allegation of breach of statutory duty is more satisfactory than one grounded on negligence alone, as the former will in most instances place a stricter duty on the defendant. As we have seen, section 47(2) of the 1974 Act does provide for civil liability unless excepted in the Regulations. Fortunately for injured parties and their lawyers, the other five sets (the Subsidiary Regulations) do not contain the exclusion found in the Head Regulations.

Employees' Duties

Before we go further it is useful to remind ourselves that there are duties on employees also, imposed by the Health and Safety at Work Act 1974, sections 7 and 8 which provide:

7. It shall be the duty of every employee while at work,

   (a) to take reasonable care for the health and safety of himself and of other persons who may be affected by his acts or omissions at work; and

   (b) as regards any duty or requirement imposed on his employer or any other person by or under any of the relevant statutory provisions, to co-operate with him so far as is necessary to enable that duty or requirement to be performed or complied with.

8. No person shall intentionally or recklessly interfere with or misuse anything provided in the interests of health, safety or welfare in pursuance of any of the relevant statutory provisions.

The Head Regulations provide in Reg. 14 (1) that

Every employee shall use any machinery, equipment, dangerous substance, transport equipment, means of production or safety device provided to him by his employer in accordance both with any training in the use of the equipment concerned which has been received by him and the instructions respecting that use which have been provided to him by the said employer by or under the relevant statutory provisions.

Reg. 14 goes on in section 2 to provide that

Every employee shall inform his employer or any other employee of that employer with specific responsibility for the health and safety of his fellow employees –

(a) of any work situation which a person with the first-mentioned employee's training and instruction would reasonably consider represented a serious and immediate danger to health and safety; and

(b) of any matter which a person with the first-mentioned employee's training and instruction would reasonably consider represented a shortcoming in the employer's protection arrangements for health and safety, insofar as that situation or matter either affects the health and safety of that first-mentioned employee or arises out of or in connection with his own activities at work, and has not previously been reported to his employer or to any other employee of that employer in accordance with this paragraph.

While, as we know, these duties do not provide a right of action in civil proceedings, the personal injury lawyer will need to keep them in mind, both in the context of contributory negligence and of vicarious liability.

We shall now go on to examine such of the Subsidiary Regulations as are relevant to tripping and slipping personal injury actions.

CHAPTER 17

Workplace (Health, Safety and Welfare) Regulations 1992

WHSW Regs

Workplace (Health, Safety and Welfare) Regulations 1992

WHSW Regs

The ACOP notes that these regulations come into effect in two stages – workplaces which are used for the first time after 31 December 1992, and modifications, extensions and conversions started after that date, should comply as soon as they are in use; existing workplaces (apart from any modifications) are covered by the regulations from 1 January 1996.

Workplaces

Reg 2[1] defined "workplace". Certain words used in the definition are themselves defined in HSWA at sections 52 and 53. The ACOP provides that "premises" means any place including an outdoor place. However "domestic premises" means a private dwelling. As the regulations do not apply to domestic premises they do not cover homeworkers; however "domestic" staff are covered in employment in sheltered accommodation, hostels and such like. Note also that a private house, or part of a house, may be converted into a workplace.

The definition of workplace includes any place within the premises to which a worker has access; thus staircases, lobbies, access or egress roads are all covered. The ACOP notes that the regulations aim to ensure that workplaces meet the health, safety and welfare needs of each member of the workforce which may include people with disabilities. The trip and slip lawyer may care to note in particular that several of the regulations require thing to be "suitable" as defined in reg. 2(3) in a way which makes it clear that traffic routes, facilities and workstations which are used by people with disabilities should be suitable for them to use. It is also worth bearing in mind in this regard that there is a British Standard on access to buildings for people with disabilities and that Building Regulations provide for making new buildings accessible to people of limited mobility, or impaired sight or hearing.

With some minor exceptions, temporary workplaces are not covered by the Regulations.

Work

"Work" means, according to the ACOP, work as an employee or self-employed person, and also work experience on certain training schemes (see the Health and Safety (Training for Employment) Regulations 1990 No. 138 reg 3).

Relevant Duties

From the viewpoint of the personal injury lawyer, the first important duty is that encountered under Regulation 4 of the WHSW Regs. This provides that every employer:

> ...shall ensure that every workplace, modification, extension or conversion which is under his control and where any of his employees work complies with any requirement of these Regulations...

So, what are these requirements in the area of tripping and slipping? The first is to be found in reg. 5.

Regulation 5

This regulation applies to maintenance of the workplace, and of equipment, devices and systems. Obviously, an unmaintained workplace can give rise to relevant hazards (broken floors, for example), as can unmaintained equipment (leaking oil, for example).

The provision is

> (1) The workplace and the equipment, devices and systems to which this regulation applies shall be maintained (including cleaned as

appropriate) in an efficient state, in efficient working order and in good repair.

(2) Where appropriate, the equipment, devices and systems to which this regulation applies shall be subject to a suitable system of maintenance.

(3) The equipment, devices and systems to which this regulation applies are –

(a) equipment and devices a fault in which is liable to result in a failure to comply with any of these Regulations

The ACOP for the WHSW Regs specifies that "efficient" in this context means efficient from the view of health, safety and welfare rather than productivity or economy.

"Equipment, devices and systems" are widely construed – they encompass, for example, lighting, fencing, lifts, escalators and so forth.

Where a defect which is potentially dangerous is discovered either it should be rectified immediately or protective measures must be taken. The example of such a measure in the ACOP is preventing access until repairs can be carried.

The ACOP gives considerable guidance on the question of maintenance. As this is likely to be relevant in many personal injury actions grounded, in whole or in part, on the civil liability arising from breach of the statutory duty imposed by the WHSW Regs. It is useful to look at this advice now.

Paragraph 22 of the ACOP notes that Reg. 5(2) requires a system of maintenance, and says that a suitable system involves ensuring that:

• regular maintenance (including, as necessary, inspection, testing, adjustment, lubrication and cleaning) is carried out at suitable intervals;

• any potentially dangerous defects are remedied and that access to defective equipment is prevented in the meantime;

• regular maintenance and remedial work is carried out properly;

• a suitable record is kept to ensure the system is properly implemented and to assist in validating maintenance programmes.

Paragraph 23 goes on to give example of equipment and devices which require a system of maintenance. Relevant to slip and trip are emergency lighting, escalators and moving walkways.

Insofar as frequency or regularity of maintenance is concerned, the following should be taken into consideration:

- type of device
- age and condition of equipment
- how used and how often used
- likelihood of defects developing
- consequences of defect
- foreseeability of defect
- manufacturers advice
- advice from other sources (e.g. HSE, British Standards etc.)

Lighting

Reg. 8 provides that workplaces should be suitably and sufficiently lit. A breach here has obvious consequences for a tripping case, for example.

Cleanliness and Waste

Reg. 9 is of particular relevance, dealing as it does with **Cleanliness and Waste Materials**. It provides:

- Every workplace and the furniture, furnishings and fittings therein shall be kept sufficiently clean;

- The surfaces of the floor, wall and ceiling of all workplaces inside buildings shall be capable of being kept sufficiently clean;

- So far as is reasonably practicable, waste materials shall not be allowed to accumulate in a workplace except in suitable receptacles.

The ACOP expressly provides in Para 68 that Reg. 9 is to be related to Reg 12(3) – avoidance of slipping, tripping and falling hazards – which is to be complied with in all cases.

The use to which the workplace is put will determine the standard of cleanliness. There is specific guidance on certain matters:

- Floors and indoor traffic routes should be cleaned at least once a week

- In workplaces where refuse accumulates, it should be removed at least daily

- More frequent cleaning may be required in some cases

- Cleaning should be carried out when necessary to clear up spillages

- Cleaning should be carried out when necessary to remove unexpected soiling

- Cleaning should be carried out by a method which does not itself create a safety risk

- Absorbent flooring liable to contamination should be sealed or coated, for example with a non-slip floor paint.

Room Dimensions and Space

Regulation 10 deals with room dimensions and space. From a trip and slip perspective ACOP 76 is particularly relevant:

> Workrooms should have enough free space to allow people to get to and from workstations and to move within the room, with ease. The number of people who may work in any particular room at any one time will depend not only on the size of the room, but on the space taken up by furniture, fittings, equipment, and on the layout of the room.

It goes on the deal with obstructions such as low beams in older buildings, which "should be clearly marked". So, presumably, should anything which might be, or cause, a tripping hazard.

Room Volume

The total volume of the room when empty, divided by the number of people normally working there, should be at least 11 cubic metres, allowing for a maximum room height of 3 metres. In tripping cases, where obstruction is a factor, the practitioner should note that the ACOP provides that the figure of 11 cubic metres is a minimum and may be insufficient if much of the room is taken up by furniture. The content and layout of the room, and the nature of the work, may require a larger figure than 11 cubic metres.

Workstations

Regulation 11 contains some provisions, enlarged upon in the ACOP, which are relevant to trip and slip situations. ACOPs 81–84 provide that:

- workstations should be arranged so that each task can be carried out safely and comfortably;

- the worker should be at a suitable height in relation to the work surface;

- work materials and frequently used equipment or controls should be within easy reach, *without undue bending or stretching* (emphasis added);

- workstations and access to workstations should be suitable for any special needs of the individual worker, including workers with disabilities;

- workstations should allow any person who is likely to work there adequate freedom of movement and the ability to stand upright;

- spells of work which unavoidably have to be carried out in cramped conditions should be kept as short as possible and there should be sufficient space nearby to relieve discomfort;

- there should be sufficient clear and unobstructed space at each workstation to enable the work to be done safely; this should allow for the manoeuvring and *positioning* of materials, for example lengths of timber (emphasis added).

Small structures, where space is by definition at a premium (such as kiosks, attendants' shelters etc.) and rooms used for lectures, meeting and similar purposes are exempt from the figure of 11 cubic metres.

Floors

Reg. 12 is unquestionably the most important regulation in WHSWR from a trip and slip viewpoint. It provides:

(1) Every floor in a workplace and the surface of every traffic route in a workplace shall be of a construction such that the floor or surface of the traffic route is suitable for the purpose for which it is used.

(2) Without prejudice to the generality of paragraph 1, the requirements in that paragraph shall include requirements that –

(a) the floor, or surface of the traffic route, shall have no hole or slope, or be uneven or slippery so as, in each case, to expose any person to a risk to his health or safety and

(b) every such floor shall have effective means of drainage where necessary

(3) So far as is reasonably practicable, every floor in a work place and the surface of every traffic route in a workplace shall be kept free from obstructions and from any article which may cause a person to trip, slip or fall.

(4) In considering whether for the purpose of paragraph (2)(a) a hole or slope exposes a person to a risk to his health or safety:

(a) no account shall be taken of a hole where adequate measures have been taken to prevent a person falling and

(b) account shall be taken of any handrail provided in connection with any slope

(5) Suitable and sufficient handrails and, if appropriate, guards shall be provided on all traffic routes which are staircases except in circumstances in which a handrail cannot be provided without obstructing the traffic route.

ACOP 89 provides, in the context of Reg. 12 that

- floor and traffic routes should be of sound construction;
- they should have adequate strength and stability taking account of the loads placed on them and the traffic passing over them.

ACOP 91 provides that:

- holes, bumps or uneven areas resulting from damage or wear and tear, *which may cause a person to trip or fall* should be made good (emphasis added);
- until they can be made good, adequate precautions should be taken against accidents, for example by barriers or conspicuous marking;
- temporary holes, for example an area where floor boards have been removed, should be adequately guarded;
- account should be taken of people with impaired or no sight.

ACOP 92 provides:

- slopes should not be steeper than necessary;
- moderate and steep slopes should be provided with a secure handrail if necessary;
- ramps used by people with disabilities should be provided with a secure handrail if necessary.

ACOP 93 provides:

- surfaces of floors and traffic routes which are likely to get wet or to be subject to spillages should be of a type which does not become unduly slippery;
- a slip-resistant coating should be applied where necessary;
- floors near to machinery which could cause injury if anyone were to fall against it (for example a woodworking or grinding machine) should be slip-resistant and be kept free from slippery substances or loose materials.

ACOP 94 provides:

- where possible, processes and plant which may discharge or leak liquids should be enclosed;

- leaks from taps or discharge points on pipes, drums and tanks should be caught or drained away;

- stop valves should be fitted to filling points on tank filling lines;

- where work involves carrying or handling liquids or slippery substances the workplace and work surfaces should be arranged in such a way as to minimise the likelihood of spillages.

ACOP 95 provides:

- where a leak or spillage occurs *and is likely to be a slipping hazard*, immediate steps should be taken to fence it off, mop it up, or cover it with absorbent granules (emphasis added).

ACOP 96 provides:

- arrangements should be made to *minimise risks from snow and ice* (emphasis added);

- this may involve gritting and snow clearing;

- this may involve closure of some routes, particularly outside stairs, ladders and walkways on roofs.

ACOP 97 provides:

- floors and traffic routes should be kept free of obstructions which may present a hazard or impede access;

- this is particularly important on or near stairs, steps, escalators and moving walkways;

- this is also important on emergency routes, in or near doorways or gangways;

- this is also important in any place where an obstruction is likely to cause an accident, for example near a corner or junction;

- where a temporary obstruction is unavoidable and is likely to be a hazard access should be prevented or steps should be taken to warn people or the drivers of vehicles of the obstruction by, for example, the use of hazard cones;

- where furniture is being moved within a workplace is should if possible be moved in a single operation;

- if it is not possible to move furniture in a single operation it should not be left in a place where it is likely to be a hazard;

- vehicles should not be parked where they are likely to be a hazard;

- materials which fall onto traffic routes should be cleared as soon as possible.

ACOP 98 provides:

- effective drainage should be provided where a floor is liable to get wet to the extent that the wet can be drained off;

- example of workplaces where this is likely to be the case are laundries, textile manufacturing (including dyeing, bleaching and finishing), work on hides and skins, potteries and food processing;

- drains and channels should be positioned so as to minimise the area of wet floor;

- the floor should slope slightly towards the drain;

- *where necessary to prevent tripping hazards* (emphasis added) drains and channels should have covers which should be as near flush as possible with the floor surface.

ACOPs 99 and 100 provide:

- every open side of a staircase should be securely fenced;

- as a minimum the fencing should consist of an upper rail at 900 mm;

- a secure and substantial handrail should be provided and maintained on at least one side of every staircase;

- however a handrail should not be provided at points where a handrail would obstruct access or egress, for example in the case of steps in a theatre aisle;

- where there is a particular risk handrails should be provided on both sides;

- examples of particular risk situations include where stairs are heavily used, or are wide, or have narrow treads *or where they are liable to be subject to spillages* (emphasis added);

- additional handrails should be provided down the centre of particularly wide staircases where necessary.

ACOPs 103, 104 and 105 provide:

- slip resistant footwear[13] may be necessary in some instances;

- local authority building regulations also have requirements on floors and stairs;

- there is a British Standard on floor construction;

- steep stairways are classed as fixed ladders (see Reg 13).

See Appendix 2[14] on footwear, shoe sole material and floor types.

Falling Objects

Reg. 13 deals with falls and falling objects, and for the most part is outside the scope of this book. However, a slip or trip may result in a fall into or onto something which may exacerbate injury. The ACOP has some relevant provisions in this context.

---

13 See *Smith* v *Scot Bowyers* (1986) *The Times* April 16 (CA) on employee's failure to renew protective footware.
14 From HSE *Slips and Trips – Guidance for Employers* 1996 (HMSO).

ACOP 106 notes:

- the consequences of falling into dangerous substances are so serious that a high standard of protection is required;

- dangerous substances in tanks, pits and other structures should be securely fenced or covered.

ACOP 108 provides:

- secure fencing should also be provided where there are factors which increase the risk of serious injury;

- such factors include where a traffic route passes close to an edge or where large numbers of people are present;

- other factors are where a person might fall onto a sharp or dangerous surface or into the path of a vehicle.

ACOP 127, 128 and 129 provide:

- slips and trips which may be trivial at ground level may result in fatal accidents when on a roof;

- it is vital therefore that precautions are taken even when access is only occasional;

- risks may be increased by moss, lichen, ice etc.;

- where regular access is needed to roofs suitable permanent access should be provided;

- where occasional access is needed to roofs other safeguards should be provided.

ACOP 132 returns to falls into dangerous substances and provides:

- every vessel containing a dangerous substance should be adequately protected to prevent a person falling into it;

- vessels installed after 31 December 1992 should be securely covered or fenced to a height of at least 1100 mm unless the sides extend to at least 1100 mm above the highest point from which people could fall into them;

- pre 1993 vessels should be at least 915 mm (exceptionally, 840 mm).

Changes of Level

A major cause of tripping injury is changes of level, particularly inside buildings. ACOP 134 provides:

- changes of level, such as a step between floors, which are not obvious should be marked to make them conspicuous.

Stacking and Racking

The main intent of this regulation is to prevent injury caused by falling objects. However, we only have to look at *Ward* v *Tesco* (where the claimant slipped on the contents of a package which had fallen from its rack) to see that it has consequences for tripping and slipping.

ACOPs 135 and 136 provide:

- materials and objects should be stored and stacked in such a way that they are not likely to fall and cause injury;

- racking should be of adequate strength and stability;

- examples are given of appropriate precautions to be taken in stacking and storage;

- some of these include safe palletisation, banding or wrapping to prevent individual articles falling out and setting limits for heights of stacks;

- other examples of precautions include regular inspection of stacks and particular instruction and arrangements for irregularly shaped objects.

Finally, from the viewpoint of tripping and slipping, ACOP 141 provides:

- when fencing or covers cannot be provided or have to be removed effective measures should be taken to prevent falls;

- access should be limited to specified people;

- others should be kept out by, for example, barriers;

- formal written permit to work system should be adopted in high risk situations.

Traffic Routes

Regulation 17 deals with the organisation of traffic routes.
Reg. 2 defined "traffic route" as:

> a route for pedestrian traffic, vehicles or both and includes any stairs, staircase, fixed ladder, doorway, gateway, loading bay or ramp.

This is an area of importance in the context of slipping and tripping and we are going to look closely at the ACOP.
ACOP 160 provides:

- there should be sufficient traffic routes to allow people on foot to circulate safely and without difficulty;

- features which obstruct routes should be avoided;

- consideration should be given to the safety of people with impaired or no sight.

ACOP 162 provides:

- access between floors should not normally be by way of ladders or steep stairs.

The comments made above in relation to tripping and slipping injury caused by objects which have fallen, rather than by falling objects *per se*, apply here also in the context of object falling from vehicles on traffic routes. In this context ACOP 163 and 164 provide:

- routes should not be used by vehicles for which they are inadequate or unsuitable;

- necessary restrictions should be clearly indicated;

- uneven or soft ground should be made smooth and firm if vehicles might otherwise overturn or shed their loads;

- sharp or blind bends should be avoided as far as possible;

- prominent warning should be given to any limited headroom;

- screens should be provided to protect people from materials which are likely to fall from vehicles;

- sensible speed limits should be set and clearly marked;

- suitable speed retarders should be provided where necessary;

- if a speed retarder is used, such as a road hump, this should be indicated by a warning sign or mark on the road.

On this last point, many tripping injuries occur on road humps and the claimant's lawyer will want to find out specifically whether this ACOP was complied with.

ACOP 166 provides:

- traffic routes used by vehicles should not pass close to anything that is likely to collapse or be left in a dangerous state if hit;

- an example given of such a thing is storage racking;

- if a vehicle is going to pass close to such a thing then adequate fencing or other protection should be provided.

Signage on traffic routes is addressed by ACOP 178 which provides:

- potential hazards should be indicated by suitable warning signs;

- hazards may include steep gradients.

Non Application

Note that WHSW regulations do not apply to:

- a workplace which is on an operational ship, boat, hovercraft, aircraft, train or road vehicle (but note reg. 13 applies to aircraft, trains and road vehicles when stationary in a workplace);

- a workplace where the only activities being undertaken are building operations or work of engineering construction (or activities in connection with same); notice an ordinary workplace can be treated as a construction site when construction work is being undertaken within it provided it is fenced off, during which time it will be excluded from the provision of these regulations;

- a workplace where the only activities being undertaken are extraction of or exploration for mineral resources;

- a workplace which is related to a mine, quarry or other mineral extraction site.

CHAPTER 18

Provision and Use of Work Equipment Regulations 1998

Provision and Use of Work Equipment Regulations 1998

Replacement of 1992 Regulations

These replace the Provision and Use of Work Equipment Regulations 1992. PUWER 1992 came into force on January 1, 1993, save for regs. 11 to 24 and 27 and Schedule 2 in so far as they applied to work equipment first provided for use in the premises or undertaking before 1st January 1993, which came into force on 1st January 1997. There will now be few cases left to which the 1992 Regulations apply. The 1998 Regulations came into force on 5 December 1998. Regulations 25 to 30 of the 1998 Regulations were subject to a transitional provision in that they did not apply to work equipment provided for use in the undertaking or establishment before 5th December 1998 until 5th December 2002.

Given that the Regulations do create civil liability, any treatment of PUWER must point out that the emphasis is on the *use of* the work equipment to which it applies. "Use" is defined widely. In this regard it is instructive to read:

Regulation 2

In these Regulations, unless the context otherwise requires..."use" in relation to work equipment means any activity involving work equipment and includes starting, stopping, programming, setting, transporting, repairing, modifying, maintaining, servicing and cleaning, and related expressions shall be construed accordingly;

"work equipment" means any machinery, appliance, apparatus or tool and any assembly of components which, in order to achieve a common end, are arranged and controlled so that they function as a whole.

Regulation 4

Suitability of work equipment

(1) Every employer shall ensure that work equipment is so constructed or adapted as to be suitable for the purpose for which it is used or provided.

(2) In selecting work equipment, every employer shall have regard to the working conditions and to the risks to the health and safety of persons which exist in the premises or undertaking in which that work equipment is to be used and any additional risk posed by the use of that work equipment.

(3) Every employer shall ensure that work equipment is used only for operations for which, and under conditions for which, it is suitable....

Regulation 5

Maintenance

(1) Every employer shall ensure that work equipment is maintained in an efficient state, in efficient working order an in good repair...

Regulation 8

Information and instructions

(1) Every employer shall ensure that all persons who use work equipment have available to them adequate health and safety information and, where appropriate, written instructions pertaining to the use of the work equipment...

Regulation 9

Training

(1) Every employer shall ensure that all persons who use work equipment have received adequate training for the purposes of health and safety, including training in the methods which may be adopted when using

the work equipment, any risks which such use may entail and precautions to be taken...

and of particular importance to trips and slips:

Regulation 12

Protection against specified hazards

(1) Every employer shall take measures to ensure that the exposure of a person using work equipment to any risk to his health or safety from any hazard specified in paragraph (3) is either prevented, or, where that is not reasonably practicable, adequately controlled.

(2) The measures required by paragraph (1) shall –

(a) be measures other than the provision of personal protective equipment or of information, instruction, training and supervision, so far as is reasonably practicable; and

(b) include, where appropriate, measures to minimise the effects of the hazard as well as to reduce the likelihood of the hazard occurring.

(3) The hazards referred to in paragraph (1) are–

(a) any article or substance falling or being ejected from work equipment...

(d) the unintended or premature discharge of any article or of any gas, dust, liquid, vapour or other substance which, in each case, is produced, used or stored in the work equipment...

Regulation 21

Lighting

Every employer shall ensure that suitable and sufficient lighting, which takes account of the operations to be carried out, is provided at any place where a person uses work equipment.

ACOP and Guidance Notes

PUWER has **guidance notes** (Notes) as well as an ACOP.

Part II of the ACOP is useful. It covers, among other topics, suitability of work equipment, maintenance, inspection, competency, installation, conditions causing deterioration and dangerous situations.

Guidance notes are intended to help identify practical ways of complying with the Regulations. They show best practice. Following the guidance is be best way of showing compliance with the Regulations; accordingly trip and slip litigators will be seeking to identify divergence.

The Guidance Notes point out that:

- PUWER amplifies and makes more explicit the general duties to provide safe plant and equipment

- virtually all the requirements already exist somewhere in the law or constitute good practice

- PUWER brings together these requirements

- PUWER cannot be looked at in isolation

- In particular, PUWER must be looked at together with MHSWR

- a common sense approach needs to be adopted to risk assessment

- this involves deciding whether the PUWER requirements are already being complied with

- the main factors to be taken into account are the severity of any likely injury likely to result from any hazard

- the likelihood of that injury happening and the numbers exposed

- there are limited areas of overlap between PUWER and WHSWR and PPE

- where there is overlap, compliance with the more specific regulation will normally be sufficient to comply with a general requirement

- the prime duty for health and safety rests with employers

- however, employees have legal duties also

- employee duties include taking reasonable care for their own health and safety and that of others who may be affected by what they do or don't do

- co-operating with their employers on health and safety

- not interfering with or misusing anything provided for their health, safety or welfare

As has been seen above, the scope of "work equipment" is extremely wide. For example:

- in addition to individual items of work equipment any assembly arranged and controlled to function as a whole is included

- an example would be a bottling plant.

It seems from this that perhaps any premises in which a whole process is carried out may itself be a piece of "work equipment" and that the provisions of PUWER ought to be applied to it as a whole. However, the structural items and the substance in the premises are specifically not "work equipment". Note that:

- livestock are not work equipment

- substances (e.g. acids, alkalis, slurry, cement, water) are not work equipment

- structural items (walls, stairs, roof) are not work equipment.

The Guidance Notes point out that the Regulations address the safety of work equipment from three aspects:

- firstly, its initial integrity
- secondly, the place where it will be used
- thirdly, the purpose for which it will be used.

Amplifying this, they say:

- equipment must be suitable by design, construction or adaptation, for the actual work it is provided to do

- in practice employers should ensure that it has been produced for the work to be undertaken

- employers should ensure that it is used in accordance with the manufacturer's specifications and instructions

- adapted equipment must be still suitable for its intended purpose

- employers must assess the location in which the work equipment is to be used

- employers must take account of any risks that may arise from the particular circumstances.

Regulation 5 deals with maintenance. This is of particular importance, particularly in relation to slipping accidents arising from leaking gaskets, poor fuel line maintenance and such like.

The Guidance Notes point out:

- firstly the HSWA obligation to carry out maintenance safely is noted;

- it is important that equipment is maintained so that its performance does not deteriorate to the extent that it puts people at risk;

- the extent and complexity of maintenance will vary enormously, from simple checks to substantial integrated programmes;

- equipment may need to be checked frequently to ensure that safety-related features are functioning correctly;

- faults in safety-critical systems may remain undetected unless maintenance procedures provide adequate inspection or testing;

- the frequency at which equipment needs to be checked is dependent on the equipment itself and the risk involved;

- any maintenance work should only be done by those who have received adequate information, instructions and training;

- the information, instructions and training should cover the reasons for the maintenance as well as the procedures and techniques that are applied;

- routine maintenance includes periodic lubrication, inspection and testing;

- routine maintenance should be based on the instructions of the manufacturer;

- routine maintenance should also take account of any specific legal requirements (such as for hoists, lifts and suchlike);

- although in most cases the combination of manufacturers' instructions and specific legal requirements would be sufficient, in particularly arduous conditions further measures may be required;

- there is no requirement for a maintenance log; however it is recommended that a record of maintenance is kept;

- this should provide information for future planning and inform maintenance personnel and others of previous action taken;

- other legislation may require records of maintenance to be provided in a specified way especially where testing is to be included.

Regulation 8

The next PUWER regulation with applicability in the context of tripping and slipping cases is Regulation 8. This regulation builds on the general duty in HSWA regarding the provision of information and instruction to employees. The claimant personal injury lawyer will, in many cases involving slips and trips in a workplace, whether such involve employees or others, want to establish whether all relevant information relating to health and safety has been made available to employees. The general requirement in MHSWR is complemented by Reg. 8 of PUWER, and of course from the claimant's point of view the fact that civil liability is not excluded under the latter is an important advantage.

This regulation can be of importance also where questions of contributory negligence arise.

The Guidance Notes say:

- information can be in writing;

- information may be verbal where this is considered sufficient;

- the employer has the responsibility of deciding whether verbal or written information is sufficient;

- information should be in writing in complicated or unusual situations;

- employee's degree of skill must be taken into account;

- employee's experience and training must be taken into account;

- the degree of supervision is relevant as is the complexity and length of the particular job;

- written instructions refer primarily to the information provided by manufacturers or suppliers such as instruction sheets or manuals;

- there are duties on manufacturers to provide sufficient information to make possible the safe installation, safe operation and maintenance of work equipment;

- employers should check such information is provided;

- employers must ensure that such information are available to those directly using and maintaining the work equipment;

- the information and written instructions should cover all the health and safety aspects of use that will arise;

- it should cover any limitations on these uses;

- it should cover *any foreseeable difficulties* (emphasis added);

- it should deal with methods of dealing with foreseeable difficulties;

- conclusions drawn from experience in the use of the equipment should be acted upon;

- such conclusions should be either recorded or steps taken to ensure that all appropriate members of the workforce are aware of them;

- all information and instructions should be presented clearly in English and/or other languages as necessary;

- instructions should be in a logical sequence with good illustrations where appropriate;

- standard symbols should be used;

- the workforce's level of training, knowledge and experience should be taken into account;

- language difficulties and disabilities will require special consideration;

- special arrangements may be needed to deal with reading difficulties or little/no understanding of English.

Regulation 9

Regulation 9 is also likely to be relevance in certain slip and trip scenarios. This regulation deals with an employer's obligation to train. The Guidance Notes say:

- the obligation to train extends not only to those who use the work equipment but also to those who supervise or manage them;

- training should be "adequate for the circumstances";

- it is impossible to lay down detailed requirements as to what constitutes "adequate training" in all circumstances;

- the shortfall between an employee's existing competence and that necessary to use, supervise or manage the use of the work equipment with due regard to health and safety will need to be evaluated;

- to be taken into account are matters such as whether the employee is to work alone, under close supervision of a competent person, or in a supervisory or management position;

- development of specific statements of what an employee needs to do and to what level will assist the employer to evaluate the extent of any shortfall in the employee's competence.

Regulation 21

Regulation 21 deals with lighting and self-evidently may have relevance in trip and slip situations. It complements the requirement for sufficient and suitable workplace lighting in WHSWR. Litigators' attention is also drawn to the advice contained in HSE guidance HS(G)38.

The Guidance Notes say:

- any place where a person uses work equipment should be suitably and sufficiently lit;

- special lighting need not be provided if the ambient lighting is suitable and sufficient for the tasks involved;

- if the perception of detail (e.g. precision measurement) is involved then additional lighting would be needed;

- local lighting may be needed;

- additional lighting should be provided in areas not covered by general lighting when work is carried out in them;

- additional lighting may be temporary or fixed;

- the standard of additional lighting will be related to the purpose for which the work equipment is being used or the work is being carried out;

• where access is foreseeable on an intermittent but regular basis consideration should always be given to the provision of permanent lighting.

Regulation 22

Regulation 22 requires that equipment is constructed or adapted in a way that takes account of the risks associated with carrying out maintenance work. The Guidance Notes say that many accidents have occurred during maintenance work, often as a result of failure to adapt the equipment to reduce the risk. From a trip and slip perspective, the possibility of slipping on spilled lubrication or drained oil or of tripping on replacement or removed parts are examples of situations which would make this regulation relevant.

The Guidance Notes point out:

• in some cases the need for safe maintenance will have been considered at the design stage and attended to by the manufacturer;

• in such cases the user will need to do little other than review the measures provided;

• in other cases users will need to consider whether any extra features need to be incorporated;

• ideally there is no risk associated with the maintenance operation;

• if however the maintenance work might involve a risk the installation should be designed so that the work can so far as is reasonably practicable be carried out with the equipment stopped.

Regulation 24

Regulation 24 deals with warnings, self-evidently of relevance in a trip and slip situation.

The Guidance Notes say:

- warnings or warning devices may be appropriate where risks to health or safety remain after other hardware measures have been taken;

- they may be incorporated into systems of work;

- they may reinforce measures of information, instruction and training;

- a warning is normally in the form of a notice or similar;

- examples are positive instructions ("non-slip footwear must be worn"), prohibitions ("no access to public"), restrictions ("do not fill sump above top level mark");

- in some cases warnings will be specified in other legislation;

- warnings can be permanent printed ones, which may be attached to or incorporated into the equipment or positioned close to it;

- portable warnings may need to be posted during temporary operations;

- in some cases words may be augmented or replaced by appropriate graphical signs;

- there is an internationally/nationally agreed set of such signs.

In the context of an agreed set of signs, litigator's attention is drawn to the Safety Signs Regulations 1980.

CHAPTER 19

Personal Protective Equipment at Work Regulations 1992 (PPE)

General   170

Personal Protective Equipment at Work Regulations 1992 (PPE)

General

These regulations came into force on 1st January 1993.
Regulation 2 says

> (1) In these Regulations, unless the context otherwise requires, "personal protective equipment" means all equipment (including clothing affording protection against the weather) which is intended to be worn or held by a person at work and which protects him against one or more risks to his health and safety, and any addition or accessory designed to meet that objective.

In a trip and slip context, footwear will be the mostly obviously relevant personal protective equipment. However, personal protective equipment which restricts movement or obstructs vision will also be pertinent (see Guidance Note 21), as will its storage.

PPE has Guidance Notes rather than an ACOP.

Note 7 says safety footwear is included in the definition of personal protective equipment.

Note 9 says:

- items such as uniforms provided for the primary purpose of presenting a corporate image are not subject to the regulations;

- the regulations do not apply to "protective clothing" provided in the food industry primarily for food hygiene purposes;

- however where any footwear or clothing protects against a specific risk to safety it will be subject to the Regulations;

- waterproof clothing (e.g. footwear) is subject to the regulations if it is worn if it is worn to protect employees against risks to health or safety but not otherwise.

Regulation 4

Regulation 4 provides:

(1) Every employer shall ensure that suitable personal protective equipment is provided to his employees who may be exposed to a risk to their health or safety while at work except where and to the extent that such risk has been adequately controlled by other means which are equally or more effective.

Reg 4 goes on to provide that personal protective equipment shall not be suitable unless –

(a) it is appropriate for the risks involved and the conditions at the place where exposure to the risk may occur;

(b) it takes account of ergonomic requirements and the state of health of the person or persons who may wear it;

(c) it s capable of fitting the wearer correctly, if necessary, after adjustments within the range for which it is designed;

(d) so far as is practicable, it is effective to prevent or adequately control the risk or risks involved without increasing overall risk;

(e) it complies with any enactment (whether in an Act or instrument) which implements in Great Britain any provision on design or manufacture with respect to health or safety in any of the relevant Community directives listed in Schedule 1 which is applicable to that item of personal protective equipment.

MHSWR require employers to assess the risks to health and safety present in the workplace. However, in a trip and slip situation, the problem of the exception of civil liability forces the practitioner to examine the other regulations' provisions in that regard very carefully. Note 20 to PPE says that these regulations should be regarded as a "last resort", after safe systems of work and engineering practices have been considered. This is not the case in a personal injury matter however – PPE may be the first place the claimant's lawyer will look.

On Reg 4 the guidance notes (**Notes 20–35**) say:

- controlling risk at source is more important than PPE as PPE protects only the person wearing it;

- theoretical maximum levels of protection are seldom achieved with PPE in practice;

- the actual level of protection is difficult to assess;

- effective protection is only achieved by suitable PPE, correctly fitted and maintained and properly used;

- PPE may restrict the wearer to some extent by limiting mobility or visibility or by requiring additional weight to be carried;

- other means of protection should therefore be used whenever reasonably practicable;

- appropriate PPE and training in its use should be provided where there is a risk to health and safety that cannot be adequately controlled by other means;

- equipment must be readily available, rather than merely on the premises;

- most PPE is provided on a personal basis but may be shared in certain circumstances;

- adequate control of the risk is the standard of protection which the PPE provided should provide;

- in some circumstances no PPE could give adequate control and it such circumstances the employer is required only to provide PPE offering the best protection practicable in the circumstances;

- use of PPE must not increase the overall level of risk;

- the nature of the job and the demands it places on workers should be taken into account when selecting PPE;

- the physical effort needed for the job, the methods of work, how long the PPE needs to be worn, requirements for visibility and communication are all matters which need to be taken into consideration;

- uncomfortable PPE is unlikely to be worn properly;

- more than one size of PPE may be needed;

- users of PPE should be consulted on selection and specification to increase the chance of its being used effectively;

- legislation implementing Community Directives must be complied with concerning the design and manufacture of PPE (e.g. Personal Protective Equipment (Safety) Regulations 1992);

- the PPE (Safety) Regs 1992 provide for certification by an independent inspection body;

- a certificate of conformity must be issued;

- with some minor exceptions, PPE must be "CE" marked.

Regulation 5

This regulation provides:

> (1) Every employer shall ensure that where the presence of more than one risk to health or safety makes it necessary for his employee to wear or use simultaneously more than one item of personal protective equipment, such equipment is compatible and continues to be effective against the risk or risks in question.

For example, certain types of safety helmets will restrict peripheral vision to an unacceptable extent when combined with safety goggles, leading to an increased risk of tripping.

Regulation 6

Reg 6 provides that an assessment must be made to determine whether the personal protective equipment is suitable, and that assessment shall include:

(a) an assessment of any risk or risks to health or safety which have not been avoided by other means

(b) the definition of the characteristics which personal protective equipment must have in order to be effective against the risks referred to in sub-paragraph (a) of this paragraph, taking into account any risks which the equipment itself may create;

(c) comparison of the characteristics of the personal protective equipment available with the characteristics referred to in sub-paragraph (b) of this paragraph.

and Reg 6 goes on to provide that any such assessment is to be reviewed if –

- there is any reason to suspect that it is no longer valid; or

- there has been a significant change in the matters to which it relates.

Note 39 states that in the simplest and most obvious cases which can easily be repeated and explained at any time, the assessment to identify suitable PPE need not be recorded. In more complex cases the assessment will need to be recorded and kept readily accessible to those who need to know the results.

Regulation 7

Regulation 7 provides that every employer shall:

> "ensure that any personal protective equipment provided to his employees is maintained (including replaced or cleaned as appropriate) in an efficient state, in efficient working order and in good repair."

Note 45 says:

- maintenance includes examination, replacement and repair;

- where appropriate records should be kept.

Regulation 8

Regulation 8 deals with accommodation for personal protective equipment and provides:

> Where an employer or self-employed person is required, by virtue of regulation 4, to ensure personal protective equipment is provided, he shall also ensure that appropriate accommodation is provided for that personal protective equipment when it is not being used.

Regulation 9

Regulation 9 deals with information, instruction and training and provides:

(1) Where an employer is required to ensure that personal protective equipment is provided to an employee, the employer shall also ensure that the employee is provided with such information, instruction and training as is adequate and appropriate to enable the employee to know–

(a) the risk or risks which the personal protective equipment will avoid or limit;

(b) the purpose for which and the manner in which personal protective equipment is to be used; and

(c) any action to be taken by the employee to ensure that the personal protective equipment remains in an effective state, in efficient working order and in good repair as required by regulation 7(1)

On Reg 9, **Note 55** say that for PPE which is simple to use and maintain, basic instruction may be all that is required.

This is likely to be the case for most PPE with trip and slip relevancy.

It may be however that, for example, anti-slip footwear may be part of a set of PPE which has more complex protective duties. In such case instruction and training might include (from **Note 55**):

- an explanation of the risks present and why PPE is needed;

- the operation, performance and limitations of the equipment;

- instructions on the selection, use and storage of PPE related to the intended use;

- factors which can affect the protection provided by PPE such as: other protective equipment, personal factors, working conditions, inadequate fitting, defects, damage and wear;

- defect and loss reporting;

- practice in putting on, wearing and removing;

- practice in inspection, testing and maintenance;

- storage instruction.

Regulation 10

Regulation 10 deals with the use of personal protective equipment:

(1) Every employer shall take all reasonable steps to ensure that any personal protective equipment provided to his employees by virtue of regulation 4(1) is properly used.

(2) Every employee shall use any personal protective equipment provided to him by virtue of these Regulations in accordance both with any training in the use of the personal protective equipment concerned which has been received by him and the instructions respecting that use which have been provided to him by virtue of regulation 9.

(3) Every self-employed person shall make full and proper use of any personal protective equipment provided to him by virtue of regulation 4(2).

(4) Every employee and self-employed person who has been provided with personal protective equipment by virtue of regulation 4 shall take all reasonable steps to ensure that it is returned to the accommodation provided for it after use.

The Guidance Notes to PPE give examples of types of safety footwear, some of which have slip and trip relevance.

Note 90 says the following are examples of types of safety footwear:

- The safety boot or shoe is the most common type of safety footwear. These normally have steel toe-caps. They may also have other safety features including *slip-resistant soles*, steel midsoles and insulation against extremes of heat and cold;

- clogs may also be used as safety footwear. They are traditionally made from beech wood which provides a good insulation against heat and absorbs shock. Clogs may be fitted with steel toe-caps and thin rubber soles for quieter tread and protection against *slippage* or chemicals;

- wellington boots protect against water and *wet conditions* and can be useful in jobs where the footwear needs to be washed and disinfected for hygienic reasons such as the food industry.

Note 91 deals with footwear for processes and activities which involve, *inter alia*, risk of slips and trips and notes in particular that **mechanical and manual handling** processes carry a risk of a fall through **slipping**.

Note 92 specifies the British and European Standards for some safety footwear, relevant examples of which are:

- BS 1870: Part 1: 1988 Specification for safety footwear other than all rubber and all plastic moulded compounds

- BS 1870: Part 3: 1981 Specification for PVC moulded safety footwear

- BS 6159: Part 1: 1987 Specification for general and industrial lined or unlined boots.

Notes 93 and 94 state:

- selection of foot protection depends primarily on the hazard;

- however, comfort, style and durability should also be considered;

- choice should be made on the basis of suitability for protection, compatibility with the work and the requirements of the user;

- safety footwear should be flexible, wet resistant and absorb perspiration;

- boots are required where ankles need protection;
- work shoes and boots should have *treaded soles for slip-resistance* (emphasis added);
- soles can be heat and oil resistant, *slip resistant* (emphasis added), shock resistant, anti-static or conductive.

Note 96 – relevant to tripping injury – states in relation to leg protection that:

- hard fibre or metal guards should be used to protect shins against impact;
- the top of the foot up to the ankle can be protected by added-on metatarsal guards.

Of relevance to slipping, **Note 97** says:

- safety footwear should be maintained in good condition;
- materials lodged into the tread should be removed.

CHAPTER 20

Manual Handling Operations Regulations 1992 (MHOR)

Manual Handling Operations Regulations 1992 (MHOR)

General

The Guidance Notes to MHOR state that more than a quarter of the accidents reported each year to the enforcing authorities are associated with manual handling, which is defined as the transporting or supporting of loads by hand or by bodily force. While strains and sprains are the most common type of injury, MHOR also addresses slipping and tripping risks. An ergonomic approach is taken, described as "fitting the job to the person, rather than the person to the job". Crude requirements such as weight limits are avoided in favour of taking into account a range of relevant factors such as the nature of the task, the load, the working environment and individual capability.

In a trip or slip case, from the claimant lawyer's perspective, MHOR should be looked at to see how the increased likelihood – and severity of consequence – of such accidents in manual handling situations is dealt with. In particular, Note 7 lists a hierarchy of measures which should have been taken by an employer, and the claimant's lawyer will want to establish whether these were complied with. The hierarchy is:

- to avoid hazardous manual handling operations so far as is reasonably practicable – this may be done by redesigning the task to avoid moving the load or by automating or mechanising the process;

- to make a suitable and sufficient assessment of any hazardous manual handling operations that cannot be avoided;

- to reduce the risk of injury from those operations so far as is reasonably practicable – particular consideration should be given to the provision of mechanical assistance but where this is not reasonably practicable then other improvements to the task, the load and the working environment should be explored.

Regulation 2

Regulation 2 needs careful attention in a slip case. It says:

"injury" does not include injury caused by any toxic or corrosive substance which–

(a) has leaked or spilled from a load;

(b) is present on the surface of a load but has not leaked or spilled from it; or

(c) is a constituent part of a load; and "injured" shall be construed accordingly.

So do MHOR have no application in a situation where, say, a worker has slipped on a pallet wet with oil which has leaked from a load? Fortunately, from our viewpoint, the Guidance Notes clarify the situation. Note 13 says:

- leak or spill hazards from toxic or corrosive *properties* (emphasis added) are not covered;

- however other properties are relevant (the example given is slipperiness caused by oil on the surface of a load).

MHOR Schedule

There is a Schedule to MHOR which sets out the factors to which the employer must have regard and questions he must consider when making an assessment of manual handling operations. In a slip and trip context the following may be relevant:

Tasks

Do they involve:

- holding or manipulating loads at a distance from trunk?
- unsatisfactory bodily movement or posture?
- excessive carrying distances?
- a rate of work imposed by a process?
- excessive pulling or pushing of the load?

The Guidance Notes elaborate on these. **Note 52** deals with holding loads at a distance from the trunk. It is clear that it is mainly concerned with back injury. From our perspective, however, holding loads at a distance from the trunk reduces forward and downward vision, increasing the likelihood of a trip. The way in which an employer has addressed this question in his assessment may therefore be relevant in a particular tripping case.

Note 62 on excessive pulling and pushing says:

> "Additionally, because of the way in which pushing and pulling forces have to be transmitted from the handler's feet to the floor, the risk of **slipping** (emphasis added) and consequent injury is much greater. For this reason pushing or pulling a load in circumstances where the grip between foot and floor is poor – whether through the condition of the floor, footwear or both – is likely to increase significantly the risk of injury."

MOHR Appendix 1

Appendix 1 contains numerical guidelines. Guideline 17 provides that the figure for pushing/pulling operations for stopping or starting a load is about 25 kg (about 250 Newtons) and for keeping the load in motion is a force of about 10 kg (about 100 Newtons); these should be reduced if the load is not between shoulder and knuckle height.

Note 71 elaborates on the foregoing in the context of team handling, noting:

- the proportion of the load borne by each will vary;

- such variation will be more pronounced on rough ground;

- additional difficulties may arise if team members impede each others' vision or movement.

Loads

Are they:

- bulky or unwieldy?
- unstable?
- difficult to grasp?

On loads, Guidance **Note 79** says:

- the bulk of the load can interfere with vision;

- where such interference cannot be avoided account should be taken of the increased risk of *slipping, tripping* (emphasis added), falling or colliding with obstructions.

Working environment

Are there

- uneven, slippery or unstable floors?
- variations in level of floors or work surfaces?
- poor lighting conditions?

On lighting, **Note 93** points out that contrast between areas of bright light and deep shadow can *aggravate tripping hazards* (emphasis added) and hinder the accurate judgement of height and distance.

Notes 145–148 deals with the nature and condition of floors, and levels, and say:

- on permanent sites a flat, well maintained and properly drained surface should be provided;

- on temporary sites the ground should be prepared if possible and kept even and firm;

- suitable covering should be provided if possible for temporary sites;

- temporary work platforms should be firm and stable;

- spillages of water, oil, soap, food scraps and other substances likely to make the floor slippery should be cleared away promptly;

- where necessary, and especially where floors can become wet, attention should be given to the choice of slip-resistant surfacing;

- where possible all manual handling operations should be carried out on a single level;

- where more than one level is involved the transition should preferably be made by a gentle slope;

- failing a gentle slope, well positioned and properly maintained steps should be provided;

- manual handling on steep slopes should be avoided as far as possible.

CHAPTER 21

Other Work Related Statutory Provisions – Factories Act 1961

Other Work Related Statutory Provisions – Factories Act 1961

The 1961 Act, section 175(5) provides:

> Any workplace in which, with the permission of or under agreement with the owner or occupier, two or more persons carry on any work which would constitute a factory if the persons working therein were in the employment of the owner or occupier, shall be deemed to be a factory for the purposes of this Act, and, in the case of any such workplace not being a tenement factory or part of a tenement factory, the provisions of this Act shall apply as if the owner or occupier of the workplace were the occupier of the factory and the persons working therein were persons employed in the factory.

Sections 28 and 29 of the Factories Act 1961 continued to apply to workplaces which existed on 31 December 1992, until 1 January 1996. WHSWR repealed sections 28 and 29 in respect of workplaces which came into use (and modifications to existing workplaces) after 31 December 1992.

Sections 28 and 29 will therefore continue to be relevant for trip and slip accidents, the cause of action for which accrued before 1 January 1996, in workplaces which existed on 31 December 1992. Obviously, as time goes on, it is less and less likely that the trip and slip litigator is going to have to be concerned with these sections.

It is provided in Section 28 that –

> All floors, steps, stairs, passages and gangways shall be of sound construction and properly maintained and shall, so far as is **reasonably practicable**, be made free from any obstruction and from any substance **likely to cause persons to slip** (*emphasis added*).

Reasonable Practicality

What is "reasonably practicable"? In *Edwards* v *National Coal Board*[15] it was said

> "Reasonably practicable" is a narrower term than "physically possible", and seems to me to imply that a computation must be made by the owner in which the quantum of risk is placed on one scale and the sacrifice involved in the measures necessary for averting the risk (whether in money, time or trouble) is placed in the other, and that, if it be shown that there is gross disproportion between them – the risk being insignificant in relation to the sacrifice – the defendants discharge the onus on them. Moreover, this computation falls to be made by the owner at a point of time anterior to the accident.

Therefore one must:

- identify the risk
- calculate the cost of averting it
- balance the risk against the cost.

That it "was not reasonably practicable" is:

- a **statutory defence** which
- must be specifically pleaded, remembering that
- a general traverse of breach of statutory duty is insufficient and
- the burden of proof lies with the defendant.

Once it is established that there is a slippery substance on a floor it is therefore for the defendants to show they have taken such reasonably practicable precautions, either to prevent its occurrence, or for its removal.

Obstructions

"Obstructions" can be minor, or indeed not what might ordinarily be understood as such. In *Gillies* v *Glywed Foundries*[16] it was held a small screw on a floor was an obstruction (although in that case it was found not practicable to keep the floor clear to the extent that such would not

---

15 *Edwards v National Coal Board* [1949] 1 KB 704.
16 *Gillies v Glywed Foundries Ltd* 1977 SLT 97.

be present). Lord Reid in *Jenkins* v *Allied Ironfounders Ltd*[17] said an obstruction was

- something present
- which served no useful purpose
- and which might cause an accident.

Water is "slippery" in the sense that it is a substance likely to cause persons to slip – see *Taylor* v *Gestetner Ltd*.[18]

Section 28

Section 28(2) provides:

> For every staircase in a building or affording a means of exit from a building, a substantial handrail shall be provided and maintained which, if the staircase has an open side, shall be on that side, and in the case of a staircase having two open sides or of a staircase which, owing to the nature of its construction or the condition of the surface of the steps or other special circumstances, such a handrail shall be provided and maintained on both sides.

Section 28(3) provides:

> Any open side of a staircase shall also be guarded by the provision and maintenance of a lower rail or other effective means.

A handrail will often prevent a slip even if there is a substance on the treads. In *Corn* v *Weirs Glass (Hanley) Ltd*[19] it was said that a rail is sufficient if it enables someone to steady themselves by grasping it.

Safe means of access

Section 29(1) provides:

> There shall, so far as is reasonably practicable, be provided and maintained safe means of access to every place at which any person has

---

17 *Jenkins* v *Allied Ironfounders Ltd* [1969] 3 All ER 1609.
18 *Taylor* v *Gestetner Ltd* [1967] 2 KIR 133.
19 *Corn* v *Weirs Glass (Hanley) Ltd* [1960] 2 All ER 300.

at any time to work, and every such place shall, so far as is reasonably practicable, be made and kept safe for any person working there.

What is the extent of the employer's duty?
An employer must

- maintain safe means of access
- so far as is reasonably practicable.

The duty does not:

- cover temporary conditions or
- cover exceptional conditions.

The case of *Levesley* v *Thomas Firth & John Brown Ltd*[20] illustrates this point.

In *Thomas* v *Bristol Aeroplane Co Ltd*[21] it was held that there is no requirement to provide for all the incidents of daily life resulting from the weather's vagaries, but this principle is limited by *Woodward* v *Renold Ltd*[22] in which case the defendants were found liable for ice on their car park because they had instituted no system whatsoever to deal with it. Ice is transient, but its occurrence may be regular.

The employers duty is owed to anyone working on the premises, including independent contractors.

20 *Levesley* v *Thomas Firth & John Brown Ltd* [1953] 1 WLR 1206.
21 *Thomas* v *Bristol Aeroplane Co Ltd* [1954] 1 WLR 694.
22 *Woodward* v *Renold Ltd* [1980] ICR 387.

CHAPTER 22

Offices, Shops and Railway Premises Act 1963; Mines and Quarries Act 1954; Construction Regulations

Offices, Shops and Railway Premises Act 1963; Mines and Quarries Act 1954; Construction Regulations

Offices, Shops and Railway Premises Act 1963

This can be thought of as the "white collar" version of the Factories Act 1961.

Sections 8 and 16 of the Offices, Shops and Railway Premises Act 1963 continued to apply to workplaces which existed on 31 December 1992, until 1 January 1996. As with sections 28 and 29 of the Factories Act 1961 above, as time passes sections 8. and 16 are less and less likely to have practical application from our perspective. WHSWR repealed sections 8 and 16 in respect of workplaces which came into use (and modifications to existing workplaces) after 31 December 1992. Sections 8 and 16 nevertheless continue to be applicable to trip and slip accidents, the cause of action for which accrued before 1 January 1996, on premises covered by this Act which existed on 31 December 1992.

The wording of section 16(1) and (2) differs from the counterpart in the Factories Act 1961 and so is reproduced here:

(1) All floors, stairs, steps, passages and gangways comprised in premises to which this Act applies shall be of sound construction and properly maintained and shall, so far as is reasonably practicable, be kept free from obstruction and from any substance likely to cause persons to slip

(2) For every staircase comprised in such premises as aforesaid, a substantial handrail or handhold shall be provided and maintained, which, if the staircase has an open side, shall be on that side; and in the case of a staircase having two open sides or of a staircase which,

owing to the nature of its construction or the condition of the surface of the steps or other special circumstances, is specially liable to cause accidents, such a handrail or handhold shall be provided and maintained on both sides.

The cases referred to in relation to the Factories Act 1961 and the various observations made refer equally to this Act.

The Mines and Quarries Act 1954

Obviously, the nature of the work undertaken in premises or areas covered by this act means that slipping and tripping is more of an "occupational hazard" than it might be in other types of employment.

"Reasonably practicality" is to the fore – for example, s.61, which provides for suitable and sufficient lighting in all parts of a mine where people work, contains an exclusion for those underground parts of a mine where lighting is inadvisable for reasons of safety.

In the context of tripping, s.34 requires that roads used by vehicles or by not less than 10 persons to walk to their work must be kept obstruction free. The surface must be kept in good repair and condition, such that it may be used with safety. Changes in gradient (and direction, height and width) should not be sudden.

Section 87(1) provides:

There shall be provided and maintained safe means of access to every place in or on a building or structure on the surface of a mine, being a place at which any person has at any time to work.

The is a considerable volume of legislation relating to mining. It is a specialist area. The HSC has a publication – *Law Relating to Safety and Health in Mines* – to which litigators are directed for further information.

Construction Regulations

There were a number of construction regulations made between 1961 and 1966, under (or continued by) the Factories Act 1961. As would appear from their title, they apply to building operations. They also apply to works of engineering construction. Both building and engineering construction must be undertaken by way of trade or business to be covered by the regulations. A "building operation" includes demolition of a building.

Regulation 6(1) of the Construction (Working Places) Regulations 1966 provides that:

> ..there shall, so far as is reasonably practicable, be suitable and sufficient safe access to and egress from every place at which any person at any time works, which access and egress shall be properly maintained.

In the case of *Byrne* v *EH Smith (Roofing)*[23] it was held that if it is reasonably foreseeable that a means of access or egress will be slippery in certain weather condition, then an employer who permits its use will be in breach of this section.

Tripping is referred to in Reg. 25(3) which says:

> Suitable measures shall be taken by the provision of adequate bevelled pieces or otherwise to reduce to a minimum the risk of tripping and to facilitate the movement of barrows where boards or planks which form part of a working platform, gangway or run overlap each other or are not of reasonably uniform thickness where they meet each other or owing to warping or for some other reason do not provide an even surface.

Slipping and tripping are the focus of Reg 30, which states:

> (1) If a platform, gangway, run or stair becomes slippery, appropriate steps shall as soon as reasonably practicable be taken by way of sanding, cleaning or otherwise to remedy the situation

> (2) Every platform, gangway, run or stair shall be kept free from any unnecessary obstruction and material and free from rubbish and any projecting nails.

Reg. 35 deals with precautions to be taken on sloping roofs.

Under the Construction (General Provisions) Regulations 1961, it is provided by Reg 48(2) that:

> [l]oose materials where not required for use shall not be placed or left so as to restrict unduly the passage of persons upon platforms, gangways, floors or other places on the site used for such passages, but shall be removed, stacked or stored so as to leave an unobstructed passage. Materials shall not be insecurely stacked...

---

23 *Byrne* v *EH Smith (Roofing)* [1973] 1 All ER 490.

The relevance of this to tripping cases will be self-evident.

CHAPTER 23

Contributory Negligence and *Res Ipsa Loquitur*

Contributory Negligence and *Res Ipsa Loquitur*

General

We deal with contributory negligence and *res ipsa loquitur* at the end of the section on accidents at work, for the reason that so many instances of such are found in the slipping and tripping cases which arise in that environment. However, the general principles can be applied to slips and trips which occur in any area.[24]

Contributory Negligence

As litigators will know, the Law Reform (Contributory Negligence) Act 1945 changed the old common law rule that any contributory negligence on the part of a claimant resulted in the defendant prevailing. Section 1(1) of the 1945 Act provides:

> Where any person suffers damage as a result partly of his own fault and partly of the fault of any other person or persons, the claim in respect of that damage shall not be defeated by reason of the fault of the person suffering the damage, but the damages recoverable in respect thereof shall be reduced to such extent as the Court thinks just and equitable having regard to the claimant's share in the responsibility for that damage.

---

24 See further and for indicative reductions, *Contributory Negligence*, Levinson, EMIS Professional Publishing, 2002.

Definition

Contributory negligence is a claimant's:

- act or omission;

- which has contributed materially to the injury; and

- which has resulted from a failure to use reasonable care for his/her own safety; and

- which the claimant ought reasonably to have foreseen would cause injury.

It should be stressed that negligent or foolhardy behaviour on the part of the claimant will only amount to contributory negligence if it to **contributed materially to the cause** of the accident.[25]

Fault

It is a fault-based concept. The 1945 Act in section 1(4) gives a definition of fault in this context:

> "Fault" means negligence, breach of statutory duty or other act or omission which gives rise to a liability or in tort would, apart from this act, give rise to the defence of contributory negligence.

Sharing the Blame

How do we apportion the fault between the parties? We do not look to the cause of the accident, but rather to the resulting injuries. An example in a tripping accident would be where a claimant had failed to wear protective clothing in a hazardous environment and, on tripping, came into unprotected contact with a dangerous substance. Here the claimant is more seriously injured than he/she otherwise would have been as a result of his/her failure and the damages will be reduced, even though the cause of the accident was not of his/her making.

---

25 *Caswell v Powell Duffryn Associated Colleries Ltd* [1940] AC 152, HL.

The general standard of care in negligence applies also to contributory negligence. However, in cases where the claimant is relying on a breach of statutory duty on the part of the defendant there is a lower standard, and thoughtlessness or forgetfulness on the part of the claimant may be excused.[26]

Risks and clear danger

Where the claimant has taken an obvious risk, this may be excused if such was occasioned by the claimant adopting a method of work sanctioned by an employer defendant. Any risk taken by a claimant which was caused by the defendant's negligence or breach of statutory duty will similarly be excused.

Ignoring clear danger in any other case is likely to amount to contributory negligence.

Disobeying Orders

A claimant employee who has failed to obey instructions, or who has actively disobeyed them, is in most cases contributorily negligent.

Res Ipsa loquitur

Although one should no longer use the latin phrase in pleadings under the CPR, this is an important maxim in the context of slipping and tripping cases grounded on common law negligence.

Where a trip or slip would not have occurred in the ordinary course of things without negligence on the part of some person other than the claimant, and the facts are such that the cause of the accident is more consistent with the defendant's negligence than any other reason, the claimant may rely on the doctrine of *res ipsa loquitur*.

The leading case is *Scott v London and St Katherine Docks Co.*[27] In that case the claimant was injured when some bags of sugar, being

---

26 See *Johns v Martin Simms (Cheltenham) Ltd* [1983] ICR 305 where a driver who inadvertently put his hand near an unguarded engine fan was excused.

27 *Scott v London and St Katherine Docks Co* Court of Exchequer Chamber [1861–73] All ER Rep 246.

lowered by means of a crane or hoist by the defendant's servants, fell on him. Earle CJ said:

> "The majority of the court have come to the following conclusion. There must be reasonable evidence of negligence, but, where the thing is shown to be under the management of the defendant, or his servants, and the accident is such as, in the ordinary course of things, does not happen if those who have the management of the machinery use proper care, it affords reasonable evidence, in the absence of explanation by the defendant, that the accident arose from want of care."

In *Barkway* v *South Wales Transport Co Ltd*[28] it was said in reference to Earl CJ's statement of the doctrine that it:

> "is dependant on the absence of explanation, and, although it is the duty of the defendants, if they desire to protect themselves, to give an adequate explanation of the cause of the accident, yet, if the facts are sufficiently known, the question ceases to be one where the facts speak for themselves, and the solution is to be found by determining whether, on the facts as established, negligence is to be inferred or not."

In tripping and slipping actions generally the best known application of the doctrine is to be found in *Ward* v *Tesco Stores Ltd*.[29] This case, which notoriously imposes an exceptionally heavy duty on shopkeepers to keep floors clean and to deal with spillages, is arguably a better illustration of *res ipsa loquitur* than it is of the duty of care. It is worth considering in some detail here. Lawton LJ said:

> On 29 June 1974, at about midday, the plaintiff went to the defendant's supermarket. It is a large one and is carried on in premises which used to be a cinema. Inside, the premises were laid out in a way which is usual nowadays in supermarkets. On duty there was a total of about 30 to 35 staff; but in the middle of the day that number was reduced because staff had to be relieved in order to enable them to get their midday meals.
>
> The plaintiff went around the store, carrying a wire basket, as shoppers are expected to do in supermarkets. She was doing her shopping at the back of the store when she felt herself slipping. She appreciated that she was slipping on something which was sticky. She fell to the ground, and sustained minor injuries. She had not seen what had caused her to slip. It was not suggested...that she had been in any way negligent in failing to notice what was on the floor as she walked along doing her shopping.

---

28 *Barkway* v *South Wales Transport Co Ltd* [1950] AC 185n.; [1950] 1 All ER 392.
29 *Ward* v *Tesco Stores Ltd* [1976] 1 All ER 219.

When she was picking herself up she appreciated that she had slipped on some pink substance which looked to her like yoghourt [sic]. Later, somebody on the defendants' staff found a carton of yoghourt in the vicinity which was two-thirds empty...This is all the plaintiff was able to prove, save for one additional fact. About three weeks later when she was shopping in the same store she noticed that some orange squash had been spilt on the floor. She kept an eye on the spillage for about a quarter of an hour. During that time nobody came to clear it up.....Those in charge of the store knew that during the course of a working week there was a likelihood of spillages occurring from time to time. It was accepted at the trial that shoppers, intent on looking to see what is on offer, cannot be expected to look where they are putting their feet. The management should have appreciated that if there are patches of slippery substances on the floor people are liable to step into them and that, if they do, they may slip. If follows too that if those are the conditions to be expected in the store there must be some reasonably effective system for getting rid of the dangers which may from time to time exist. The only precautions which were taken were, first, the system of having the floor brushed five or six times during the working day and, secondly, giving instructions to the staff that if they saw any spillage on the floor they were to stay where the spill had taken place and call somebody to clean it up.....In this case the floor of the supermarket was under the management of the defendants and their servants. The accident was such as in the ordinary course of things does not happen if floors are kept clean and spillages are dealt with as soon as they occur. If an accident does happen because the floors are covered with spillage, then in my judgment some explanation should be forthcoming from the defendants to show that the accident did not arise from any want of care on their part: and in the absence of any explanation the judge may give judgement for the plaintiff.

The court was not unanimous. Ormrod LJ dissented and Megaw LJ felt accordingly constrained to add some words in support of Lawton LJ's judgment:

...It is for the plaintiff to show that there has occurred an event which is unusual and which, in the absence of explanation, is more consistent with fault on the part of the defendants than the absence of fault; and to my mind the learned judge was wholly right in taking that view of the presence of this slippery liquid on the floor of the supermarket in the circumstances of this case: that is that the defendants knew or should have known it was a not uncommon occurrence; and that if it should happen, and should not be promptly attended to, it created a serious risk that customers would fall and injure themselves. When the plaintiff has established that, the defendants can still escape from liability. They could escape from liability if they could show that the accident must have happened, or even on the balance of probability would have been likely to have happened, irrespective of the existence of a proper and adequate system, in relation to the circumstances, to provide for the safety of customers. But, if the defendants wish to put forward such a case, it is for them to show that, on the balance of probability, either by evidence or by inference from the evidence that is given or is not given, this accident would have been at least equally likely to have happened despite a proper system designed to give reasonable protection to customers. That, in this case, they wholly failed to do...

In *Balachandra v Southampton and South West Hampshire Health Authority*[30] where a drink had been spilled on the steps of a hospital, and the claimant slipped thereon and was injured, the Court of Appeal held that the trial judge had been entitled to arrive at his finding of negligence on the basis that the spill self-evidently had not been dealt with immediately. In that case there was a finding of 60% contributory negligence on the part of the claimant.

---

30 *Balachandra v Southampton and South West Hampshire Health Authority* (CA) unreported January 23 1996.

CHAPTER 24
Bibliography/Resources

Bibliography/Resources

Clerk and Lindsell on Torts (18th ed) Sweet & Maxwell, ISBN: 0–421–76260–8.

Code of Practice for Maintenance Management (Delivering Best Value in Highway Maintenance), IHT, 2001.

Foster, C, *Tripping and Slipping Cases: A Practitioner's Guide (3rd ed.)* Sweet & Maxwell 2002.

Government Statistical Service, *Health and Safety Statistics 1995/1996* (HMSO, 1996).

Health and Safety Executive, *Preventing Slips, Trips and Falls at Work* (HSE, 1996).

Health and Safety Executive, *Slips and Trips – Guidance for Employers* (HMSO, 1996).

Health and Safety Executive, *Slips and Trips – Guidance for the Food Processing Industry* (HMSO, 1996).

Morrell J and Foster R, eds. *Local Authority Liability*, Jordans 1998 ISBN 0–85308–509–9.

Orlik, M *An Introduction to Highway Law*, Shaw & Sons Limited 1996.

Sauvain, S.J., *Highway Law* (2nd ed.), Sweet & Maxwell 1997 ISBN 0–421–562307.

Zindani, *Health and Safety: A Modern Guide* EMIS Professional Publishing 2002 ISBN 1–85811–217–6.

Steiner, J, Enforcing EC Law, Blackstone Press: London, 1995.

Rogers, W V H, *Winfield & Jolowicz on Tort* (16th ed.) Sweet & Maxwell, ISBN: 0–421–76850–9.

Appendices

APPENDIX 1

Sources of Information and Expert Witnesses

Organisations

Health and Safety Laboratory, Broad Lane, Sheffield S3 7HQ
Tel: 0114 892000

British Standards Institution, 389 Chiswick High Road, London W4 4AL
Tel: 0208 996 9001

Royal Society for the Prevention of Accidents, Edgbaston Park, 353 Bristol Road, Birmingham B5 7ST
Tel: 0121 248 2000

British Retail Consortium, Bedford House, 69–79 Fulham High Street, London SW6 3JW
Tel: 0207 233 1489

British Cleaning Council, 15 Fairfield Lane, Wolverley, Nr Kidderminster, Worcester DY11 5Q
Tel: 01562 850704

Building Research Establishment, Garston, Watford WD2 7JR
Tel: 01923 664000

Published guidance and research reports/British and European Standards

Details of relevant British and European standards are available from the British Standards Institution (address above), these include:

BS 1711 1974 (1991) Specification for Solid Rubber Flooring
ISBN 0 58008526 0

BS 2592 1973 (1991) Specification for Thermoplastic Flooring Tiles
ISBN 0 58007926 0

BS 3260 1969 (1991) Specification for Semi-flexible PVC flooring
ISBN 0 58005158 0

BS 3261 1973 (1991) Specification for Unbacked Flexible PVS flooring
ISBN 0 58007701 2

BS 8204 Part 3 1993 In situ Flooring. Code of Practice for Polymer Modified
Cementitous Wearing Surfaces
ISBN 0 58022149 0

BS 8204 Part 4 1993 In situ Floorings. Code of Practice for Terrazzo Wearing
Surfaces
ISBN 0 58022452 X

BS 5378 1982 Safety signs and colours

> Part 1 1980 ISBN 0 58011506 2
> Part 2 1980 ISBN 0 58011507 0
> Part 3 1982 ISBN 0 58012779 6

Guidance Slips and Trips: Guidance for the Food Processing Industry

HS(G) 156 1996 HSE Books ISBN 0 7176 0832 8

Workplace health, safety and welfare.
Approved Code of Practice and Guidance

L24 1992 HSE Books ISBN 0 7176 0413 6

Management of health and safety at work. Approved code of Practice L21 1992
ISBN 0 71760412 8

Personal protective equipment at work. Guidance on Regulations L25 1992
HSE Books
ISBN 0 71760415 2

5 Steps to risk assessment IND(G)163L 1994 HSE Free leaflet

Five steps to successful health and safety management IND(G)132L 1992
HSE Free leaflet

Essentials of health and safety at work 1995 HSE Books
ISBN 0 71760716 X

HSE priced and free publications are available by mail order from HSE Books.

HSE priced publications are also available from good booksellers.

Research reports and articles

Harris GW and Shaw S R, 1988, "*Slip Resistance of Floors. User's Opinions, Tortus Instrument Readings and Roughness Measurements,*" J Occup, Accid 9 (1988) 287–298

Holah J, 1994, "*Hygiene and Safety in the Food Industry; Compromise or Complementary*". Conference proceedings Paper 7 of Slipping – Towards Safer Flooring RAPRA, Shrewsbury, UK ISBN 1 85957 0259

Manning D P, Jones C and Bruce M, (1985) "*Slip-resistance on Icy Surfaces of Shoes*", "*Crampons and Chains – A new machine*" J. Occup.Accid 7 (1986) 273–283

Redfern M S and Bidana B, (1994), "*Slip Resistance of the Shoe-Floor Interface under Biomedically Relevant Conditions*" Ergonomics 37 No 3 (1994) 511–524

Other useful addresses

Association of Personal Injury Lawyers (APIL), 11 Castle Quay, Nottingham
NG7 1FW
0115 958 0585

Association of Trial Lawyers of America (ATLA), 1050 31st Street NW,
Washington DC 20007, USA
001 202 965 3500

British Safety Council, 70 Chancellors Road, London W6 9RS
0208 741 1231

Health and Safety Executive, Magdalen House, Stanley Precinct, Bootle
L20 3QZ
0151 951 4000

Institute of Highway Incorporated Engineers, 20 Queensbury Place, London
SW7 2DR
0207 823 9093

Institute of Civil Engineers, 1–7 Great George Street, London SW1P 3AA
0207 222 7722

Insitution of Structural Engineers, 11 Upper Belgrave Street, London
SW1X 8BH
0207 235 4535

Met Office, London Road, Bracknell, Berkshire RG12 2SZ
01344 856038

Society of Operations Engineers (formerly Institute of Road Transport
Engineers), 22 Greencoat Place, Westminster, London S1P 1PR
0207 630 1111

APPENDIX 2

Slip Controls

Practitioners should consult this table when evaluating the causative factors in any slipping case, and in particular when considering the controls and preventative measures which may have been taken in a slip-at-work case. The information in this and the following two appendices have been reproduced by permission of the HSE. A full text is available at *www.hse.gov.uk/pubns/fiso6.pdf*.

Table 1 Slips risks controls

Causative factors	Practical measures for slips risk control
ENVIRONMENTAL FACTORS	
(a) Contamination of the floor Eg from: • spillages • wet cleaning methods • shoes • water and grease laden vapour (poor ventilation) • natural contamination such as wet, and/or mud in outside areas • dry contamination, eg polythene bags left on floors, product spillages or cardboard laid over spills	(1) **Eliminate contamination in the first place** Eg maintain equipment to prevent leakage, enclose transfer systems, cover outside areas, use dry methods for cleaning floors If not reasonably practicable: (2) **Prevent contamination becoming deposited on to walking surfaces** Eg by lids on portable vessels, lips around tables, bunds around equipment, drip drays under taps, cleaning incoming footwear, using effective extraction ventilation of fumes and steam with grease filtration If not reasonably practicable: (3) **Limit the effects of contamination** • by immediate treatment of spillages • by safe cleaning methods, minimising and drying wet floors

- by prompt repair of leaks
- by limiting the area of contamination, eg by the location of drainage channels

If there is still a risk:

(b) Inherent slip resistance of the floor not maintained adequately

Eg from incorrect or inadequate cleaning or maintenance or wear.

(4) Maximise the surface roughness and slip resistance of the existing floor surface

Eg follow an effective cleaning regime as indicated by the floor supplier. Find out from suppliers the correct cleaning regime to remove even thin layers of contamination and cleaning agent residue; and ensure the regime is repeated often enough and adhered to

- Train, supervise and equip those who clean floors to ensure effective and safe cleaning. Frequent spot cleaning can supplement whole-floor cleaning
- Maintain floors and drainage to maximise slip resistance

If this is not enough:

(c) The slip resistance of the floor is too low

This is influenced by:

- surface roughness of floor
- the friction between the floor and shoe
- the sharpness of the granular microsurface peaks
- the shape and height of ridges in the floor surface if profiled
- the drainage capacity of the floor
- the hardness of the floors
- incorrect installation of the floor

(5) Increase the surface roughness of the existing floor

Eg stick-on anti-slip strips, matting, treatments and abrading that increase slip resistance

If this is still not enough:

(6) Lay a more slip resistant floor with higher surface roughness

In a few cases a new floor may be needed:

(1) Draw up a specification for the supplier to meet. Experience of how that floor performs in a similar situation will be the best guide

(2) Select a floor with sufficient surface roughness. Floors with a rough surface, and, if appropriate, profiles to drain the wet away, are best for wet conditions

(3) Provide effective drainage – profiles, channels etc

(4) See the installation is correctly done

(5) Check to see the specification has been met

(Note: research has shown rough floors can be cleaned to the same level of cleanliness as smooth floors and should not conflict with food hygiene requirements but you should recognise that meeting both safety and hygiene requirements might require more cleaning effort and special equipment) and:

(d) Steps and slopes: do they cause sudden changes in step or not offer adequate foot hold and/or hand hold?

(7) **See steps and slopes give adequate foot and hand hold and have no sudden changes**

Eg remove sudden changes in levels and see steps have clearly visible nosings, good hand holds etc.

and:

(e) Adverse conditions hiding the floor conditions and distracting attention

Eg

- low light levels
- shadows
- glare
- excess noise
- extreme temperature
- bulky/awkward personal protective equipment

(8) **See the prevailing conditions allow good visibility of and concentration on floor conditions**

Eg provide adequate lighting, and see environmental demands do not distract attention from the floor condition

and:

ORGANISATIONAL FACTORS

(f) The nature of the task Eg • the need to carry, lift, push, lower or pull loads • the need to turn, to move quickly or take long strides • distractions • having no hands free to hold on to break a fall	**(9) Analyse the tasks to see no more than careful walking is required in any slip risk area** Tasks should not compromise ability to walk safely. Tasks should be: • mechanised to avoid the need for pushing, lifting, carrying, pulling etc while walking on a slippery floor • moved to safer areas • slowed so operators do not have to hurry and:
(g) Placing vulnerable individuals Eg • poor knowledge of risks and measures • poor health and agility • poor eyesight • fatigue	**(10) Allocate tasks in slips risks areas only to those competent to follow slips precautions** and:
(h) Insufficient supervision	**(11) Supervise to monitor physical controls and to see safe practices are followed** and:
(i) Safety culture which is not supportive	**(12) Establish a positive attitude that slips risks can be controlled** and:

PERSONAL PROTECTIVE EQUIPMENT: SHOE FACTORS

(j) Shoes offer insufficient slip resistance in combination with the floor surface, because of • type of shoe • sole material • contamination of shoes • sole pattern • wear • fit • maintenance/renewal	(13) Select suitable shoes for the floor, environment and the individual Base this on experience. Microcellular urethane and rubber soles are the least slippery on level wet floors. Get employees to maintain the shoe soles in good repair and keep them free from contamination. Replace them before they have worn smooth and:

INDIVIDUAL FACTORS

(k) Unsafe action from staff Eg from lack of: • awareness of the risk • knowledge of how slips occur • information and training or • distraction, carelessness	(14) Train, inform and supervise employees Eg on the risk, the control arrangements and employees role(s), especially to: • clean as they go • report contamination • maintain footwear • walk appropriately to circumstances (15) Set procedures for visitors

APPENDIX 3
Trip Controls

Practitioners should consult this table when evaluating the causative factors in any tripping case, and in particular when considering the controls and preventative measures which may have been taken in a trip-at-work case.

Table 2 Trips risks controls

Causative factors	Practical measures for trips risk control
ENVIRONMENTAL FACTORS	
(a) Uneven surfaces Eg gulleys, holes, steps	**(1) Eliminate holes, slopes or uneven surfaces which could cause trips risks** Eg inspect and maintain floors so they have a smooth finish and no holes to cause a tripping hazard. Highlight any changes in level and make slopes gradual and steps clearly visible, avoid open gulleys and channels and:
(b) Obstructions Eg accumulation of articles such as work in progress or waste	**(2) Good housekeeping** **(a) Eliminate materials likely to obstruct and cause trips** Eg analyse work flows and design process so waste and product does not accumulate or if this is not reasonably practicable:

(b) **Prevent material obstructing**

Eg provide sufficient suitable receptacles for work in progress, correctly sited; mark out walkways, working areas and receptacle locations and make sure they are kept free of obstruction

and:

(c) **Adverse environment**

Eg inadequate illumination to see floor properly, or glare

(3) **Provide suitable lighting to permit obstructions to be seen**

and:

ORGANISATIONAL FACTORS

(d) **The nature of the task creates obstructions**

(4) **Analyse the tasks** and process flows to see if the work can be handled to eliminate or minimise obstructions

and:

(e) **Safety culture which is not supportive**

(5) **Establish a positive attitude that trips can be prevented**

INDIVIDUAL FACTORS

(f) **Safe practices not followed**

and:

(7) **Train, inform and supervise** employees

APPENDIX 4
A. Checklist/ Slip or Trip at Work
B. Slip and Trip Prevention – Dealing with Hazards

A.   Practitioners should investigate whether employers have properly managed the control of slip and trip hazards by finding out the answers to these questions (which are addressed to the employer):

Have you: **Comments**

Planned how you will manage the control of these hazards?

- Identified the significance (and cost) to you of slip and trip injuries or the potential savings that could be made?

- Identified where and to whom the more significant risks occur, both on and off site?

- Identified the sources of contamination and their contributory causes, in each case?

- Assessed the situation to see if more control measures are needed?

- Planned what control measures are needed (see "Implemented the controls against slips risks?" below)

- Recorded your arrangements to manage the risks, including planning, organising, controlling, monitoring and review?

- Secured commitment to reduce these injuries and set an objective to aim for?

Organised to implement your plan?

- Appointed a 'competent' assistant?

- Consulted safety representatives?

- Allocated responsibilities, such as for inspection, investigation, maintenance and vetting of new plant?

- Given training?

- Set up communication systems for slip and trip risks controls?

Implemented the controls against slip risks?

- Identified the source of contamination?

- Eliminated it?

- Prevented it reaching the floor?

- Or, if that is impossible, limited the spread of contamination and arranged for it to be cleared up and dried immediately, repeating this as often as necessary?

- Obtained the specification of the correct cleaning regime and the set cleaning tasks?

- Trained, equipped and supervised the floor cleaning staff?

- Set up arrangements to identify and attend to maintenance needs on floor and equipment?

- Increased the slip resistance of existing flooring?

- If the slip resistance is still inadequate, have you considered replacing the floor surface with one that is sufficiently slip resistant?

- Made sure that there are no sudden changes of slope, level, surface or step and, if there are, taken other measures to achieve safety?

- Made sure that lighting and other environmental items are adequate, so that contamination can be seen?

- Analysed tasks and, if necessary, changed working practices to eliminate the need for staff to move quickly or awkwardly in any remaining slip risk area?

- In potentially slippery areas, only given tasks to staff who are competent to deal with the remaining risks?

- Provided effective supervision?

- Demonstrated commitment to the reduction of slip injuries?

- Provided where necessary, suitable slip resistant shoes?

- Made arrangements for shoes to be kept free from contamination, and for them to be replaced before wearing smooth?

- Informed and trained staff on the importance of being aware of risk, to watch the way they walk, and to report and clean up spillages promptly, including cleaning floors?

- Set procedures for visitors and delivery staff?

Implemented the controls against trip risks?

- Eliminated uneven surfaces where necessary?

- Examined process flow to eliminate work in progress or the accumulation of waste?

- Provided enough suitable receptacles for any material?

- Marked walkways and receptacle locations?

- Set up systems of inspection and maintenance, to detect the need for floor repairs?

- Provided suitable lighting above floors?

- Analysed tasks to reduce the risk of obstructions being created?

- Demonstrated commitment to a reduction of trip injuries?

- Provided effective supervision?

- Informed and trained operators?

Monitored and reviewed your progress?

- Identified the information you need to collect to monitor the effectiveness of the arrangements?

- Set up arrangements to monitor and review progress?

- Set up arrangements to review the assessment periodically?

B.   Practitioners should find out whether the appropriate preventative measures, as set out below, were taken in any particular case:

Hazard	*Suggested action*
Spillage of wet and dry substances	Clean spills up immediately. If a liquid is greasy ensure a suitable cleaning agent is used. After cleaning the floor may be wet for some time. Use appropriate signs to tell people the floor is still wet and arrange alternative bypass routes.
Trailing cables	Position equipment to avoid cables crossing pedestrian routes, use cable covers to securely fix to surfaces, restrict access to prevent contact.
Miscellaneous rubbish, example plastic bags.	Keep areas clear, remove rubbish and do not for allow to build up.
Rugs/mats	Ensure mats are securely fixed and do not have curling edges.
Slippery surfaces	Assess the cause and treat accordingly, for example treat chemically, appropriate cleaning method etc.
Change from wet to dry floor surface	Suitable footwear, warn of risks by using signs, locate doormats where these changes are likely.
Poor lighting	Improve lighting levels and placement of light fittings to ensure more even lighting of all floor areas.
Changes of level	Improve lighting, add apparent tread nosings.
Slopes	Improve visibility, provide hand rails, use floor markings.

Smoke/steam obscuring view	Eliminate or control by redirecting it away from risk areas; improve ventilation and warn of it.
Unsuitable footwear	Ensure workers choose suitable footwear, particularly with the correct type of sole.
	If the type of work requires special protective footwear the employer is required by law to provide it free of charge.

APPENDIX 5

Footwear

Practitioners may find the following, reproduced by permission from the HSE's *Slips and Trips – Guidance for Employers* (HMSO 1996), of use when assessing whether an employee had been provided with appropriate PPE:

1. British and European Standards for safety footwear do not include test specifications for slip resistance. Safety footwear is not designed primarily to protect the wearer from slipping. Its main aim is to protect the foot from falling objects, protruding nails, etc.

2. Choosing suitable footwear to prevent slips needs care. Different characteristics are needed for different conditions. The sole of the footwear will work in much the same way a car tyre i.e.;

    • On wet surfaces the sole should have a well defined pattern (tread) as more edges will give a firmer grip. The tread will cut through surface liquid and break up the slippery layer under foot.

    • On dry surfaces it is better to have as much of the sole as possible in contact with the ground so the pattern on the sole is less important.

3. It is not possible to make firm recommendations about soling materials as none will perform well in all conditions. The best approach is to test a range of footwear under actual working conditions to find which is best in the particular circumstances. New soles may have a skin or film on them from the moulding or forming process. Once this has worn off the anti-slip performance of the soles will change. Footwear should therefore be tried over a period of time.

4. Some combinations of shoe sole and flooring materials have been found to be less slippery than others. The following table may help with the choice of footwear.

Shoe sole material and floor types

Slip resistance of combinations

Normal floor conditions	Floor types	Shoe sole materials		
		PVC and leather	Urethane and rubbers	Microcellular urethane and rubbers
Smooth	Stainless steel	Most slippery	Most slippery	Less slippery
	Polished ceramic	Most slippery	Most slippery	Less slippery
	Polished wood	Most slippery	Most slippery	Less slippery
	Smooth resin	Most slippery	Most slippery	Less slippery
Matt	Matt ceramic	Most slippery	Less slippery	Less slippery
	Terrazzo	Most slippery	Less slippery	Least slippery
	PVC/vinyl	Less slippery	Less slippery	Least slippery
	Concrete	Less slippery	Least slippery	Least slippery
Rough	Paving Stones	Less slippery	Least slippery	Least slippery

Relative slip resistance of combinations of shoes and floors in water-wet conditions

Key: Most slippery   Less slippery   Least slippery

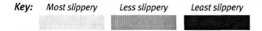

Each floor listed is untreated, is not profiled and is in water-wet conditions. Slipperiness may be increased by other liquids, especially those more viscous than water.

With wear, floors and shoe soles may change, often becoming more slippery. However, microcellular urethanes often remain unchanged with wear.

APPENDIX 6

Occupiers' Liability Acts (Extracts)

Occupiers' Liability Act 1957

2.— (1) An occupier of premises owes the same duty, the "common duty of care", to all his visitors, except in so far as he is free to and does extend, restrict, modify or exclude his duty to any visitor or visitors by agreement or otherwise.

(2) The common duty of care is a duty to take such care as in all the circumstances of the case ise reasonable to see that the visitor will be reasonably safe in using the premises for the purposes for which he is invited or permitted by the occupier to be there.

(3) The circumstances relevant for the present purpose include the degree of care, and of want of care, which would ordinarily be looked for in such a visitor, so that (for example) in proper cases

(a) an occupier must be prepared for children to be less careful than adults; and

(b) an occupier may expect that a person, in the exercise of his calling, will appreciate and guard against any special risks ordinarily incident to it, so far as the occupier leaves him free to do so.

(4) In determining whether the occupier of premises has discharged the common duty of care to a visitor, regard is to be had to all the circumstances, so that (for example)–

(a) where damage is caused to a visitor by a danger of which he had been warned by the occupier, the warning is not to be treated without more as absolving the occupier from liability, unless in all the circumstances it was enough to enable the visitor to be reasonably safe: and

(b) where damage is caused to a visitor by a danger due to the faulty execution of any work of construction, maintenance or repair by an independent contractor employed by the occupier, the occupier is not to be treated without more as answerable for the danger if in all the circumstances he had acted reasonably in entrusting the work to an independent contractor and had taken such steps (if any) as he reasonably ought in order to satisfy himself that the contractor was competent and that the work had been properly done.

(5) The common duty of care does not impose on an occupier any obligation to a visitor in respect of risks willingly accepted as his by the visitor (the question whether a risk was so accepted to be decided on the same principles as in other cases in which one person owes a duty of care to another).

(6) For the purposes of this section, persons who enter premises for any purpose in the exercise of a right conferred by law are to be treated as permitted by the occupier to be there for that purpose, whether they in fact have his permission or not.

Occupiers' Liability Act 1984

1.— (1) The rules enacted by this section shall have effect, in place of the rules of the common law, to determine–

   (a) whether any duty is owed by a person as occupier of premises to persons other than his visitors in respect of any risk of their suffering injury on the premises by reason of any danger due to the state of the premises or to things done or omitted to be done on them; and

   (b) if so, what that duty is.

(2) For the purposes of this section, the persons who are to be treated respectively as an occupier of any premises (which, for those purposes, include any fixed or movable structure) and as his visitors are–

   (a) any person who owes in relation to the premises the duty referred to in section 2 of the Occupiers' Liability Act 1957 (the common duty of care), and

   (b) those who are his visitors for the purposes of that duty.

(3) An occupier of premises owes a duty to another (not being his visitor) in respect of any such risk as is referred to in subsection (1) above if–

   (a) he is aware of the danger or has reasonable grounds to believe that it exists;

   (b) he knows or has reasonable grounds to believe that the other is in the vicinity of the danger concerned or that he may come into the vicinity of the danger (in either case, whether the other has lawful authority for being in that vicinity or not); and

   (c) the risk is one against which, in all the circumstance of the case, he may reasonably be expected to offer the other some protection.

(4) Where, by virtue of this section, an occupier of premises owes a duty to another in respect of such a risk, the duty is to take such care as is reasonable in all the circumstances of the case to see that he does not suffer injury on the premises by reason of the danger concerned.

(5) Any duty owed by virtue of this section in respect of a risk may, in an appropriate case, be discharged by taking such steps as are reasonable in all the circumstances of the case to give warning of the danger concerned or to discourage persons from incurring the risk.

(6) No duty is owed by virtue of this section to any person in respect of risks willingly accepted as his by that person (the question whether a risk was so accepted to be decided on the same principles as in other cases in which one person owes a duty of care to another).

(7) No duty is owed by virtue of this section to persons using the highway, and this section does not affect any duty owed to such persons.

(8) Where a person owes a duty by virtue of this section, he does not, by reason of any breach of the duty, incur any liability in respect of any loss of or damage to property.

(9) In this section–

   "highway" means any part of a highway other than a ferry or waterway;

   "injury" means anything resulting in death or personal injury, including any disease and any impairment of physical or mental condition; and

   "movable structure" includes any vessel, vehicle or aircraft.

APPENDIX 7

Precedents

Precedents in IT form and hard copy are widely available, and will be to hand in most personal injury lawyers' offices. Whether to include any at all in this text was the subject of some deliberation. Ultimately, a decision was made to include the following, by way of illustration only. Practioners should compare them with standard precedents before relying upon them.

A. Highway Trip

IN THE STOKESHIRE COUNTY COURT **Case No.   /2003**

BETWEEN

Alf Faller **Claimant**

and

Stokeshire County Council **Defendant**

1. On the   day of   200   in daylight hours the Claimant was walking on the pavement outside the door of 21 College Crescent Oldtown Stokeshire ("the highway") when he tripped on a defect in the said pavement and was so caused to fall.

2. The defect in the said pavement took the form of one corner of the paving stone in the centre of the pavement standing proud of its surrounding paving stones by approximately 3.9 centimetres (one and one half inches statute measure) at its highest point of protrusion, the protrusion being occasioned by a depression apparent underneath the centre of the paving

stone which had caused the paving stone to crack in the middle and sink, with a consequent raising of the edge of the said paving stone.

3. The Defendant is and was at all material times the highway authority with a duty to maintain the highway known as College Crescent Oldtown Stokeshire.

4. The Claimant's accident was caused by the Defendant's breach of the statutory duty to repair or maintain the highway imposed upon it by the Highways Act 1980 s.41.

5. Further or in the alternative the said accident was caused by the negligence of the Defendant.

6. Further or in the alternative the said accident was caused by a nuisance which was caused or permitted by the Defendant.

Particulars of breach of statutory duty and/or negligence

a) Failing adequately or at all to maintain and/or repair the highway

b) Failing to maintain the level of the said paving stone on the highway to that of the surrounding paving stones or to replace it.

c) Failing to otherwise render the highway safe for pedestrians to use and to safely pass and repass upon and along it.

d) Failing to rail off the defect or to erect fencing around it or to erect a hoarding or to take other measures to prevent access to the defect.

e) Failing to give any warning of the defect by way of notices, signs, safety devices or otherwise

nnn) *Insert here any details of other instances of similar accidents at or nearby to the defect, or records of any complaints made to the authority, known to the Claimant.*

7. The Claimant will say that the fact and the circumstances of the accident speak for themselves and are themselves evidence of negligence and breach of statutory duty of the Defendants.

8. By reason of the matters aforesaid the Claimant who was born on the 6 June 1956 sustained injuries, loss and damage.

B. Retail Premises Slip

IN THE STOKESHIRE COUNTY COURT   **Case No.**   **/2003**

BETWEEN

Alf Faller   **Claimant**

and

Acme Supermarket Limited   **Defendant**

1.   The Defendant is and was at all material times the owner and occupier of premises known as Acme Supermarket Limited of College Road, Sheltown, Stokeshire ST1 2DD, a supermarket premises (the supermarket).

2.   On the   day of   200   the Claimant entered the supermarket as a lawful visitor under the Occupiers Liability Act 1957 (the Act) and as such was owed a duty of care pursuant to the said Act.

3.   The Claimant was walking down the rear aisle of the supermarket, when he slipped on a quantity of bacon brine lying on the floor which had dripped from a cold storage cabinet.

4.   As a result of the slip the Claimant fell to the floor, landing on his lower back.

5.   The said accident was caused by the negligence and/or breach of statutory duty under the Occupiers Liability Act 1957, s.2 of the Defendant, its servants or agents.

Particulars of negligence and/or breach of statutory duty

(a) Causing or permitting the bacon brine to be upon the floor and to consitute a danger and a trap to persons lawfully using the premises

(b) Failing to immediately clear up the said bacon brine

(c) Failing to institute and/or maintain any or any adequate system for the regular inspection of the floor of the supermarket and the removal therefrom of anything likely to cause harm

(d) Allowing the Claimant to walk over a floor surface which was in a dangerous ???

(e) Failing to give any proper warning, orally or by notice in writing or otherwise, to visitors of the danger posed by the presence of the bacon brine.

(f) Allowing the floor to remain in a dangerous condition.

(g) Failing to take any or any reasonable care to ensure that the Claimant was reasonably safe in using the supermarket as a visitor.

(h) Failing to take any or adequate precautions for the safety of the Claimant.

(i) Exposing the Claimant to a risk of damage/injury of which they knew or ought to have known.

5. The Claimant will say that the fact and the circumstances of the accident speak for themselves and are themselves evidence of negligence and breach of statutory duty of the Defendants

6. By reason of the matters aforesaid the Claimant, who was born on 6 June 1956, sustained personal injuries, loss and damage

C. Trip at work

IN THE STOKESHIRE COUNTY COURT Case No. /2003

BETWEEN

Alf Faller Claimant

and

Stokeshire Widgets plc Defendant

PARTICULARS OF CLAIM

Concise statement of facts

1   At all material times the claimant was employed as a widget-maker by the Defendant company at its manufacturing premises at Main Street Oldtown Stokeshire SK1 1KS.

2   On or about the   day of   200   whilst in the course of that employment the claimant was walking along a path which led from the outdoor widget pre-assembly storage bins to the company canteen. There was a pothole in the path. The Claimant tripped in the pothole and fell, and as a consequence he sustained injury.

Legal principles relied upon

3   The Workplace (Health, Safety and Welfare) Regulations 1992 applied to the Defendant's premises, and in consequence the Defendant was in breach of the following statutory duties:

(a) contrary to regulation 12(2)(a) of the Workplace (Health, Safety and Welfare) Regulations 1992 the path was a traffic route which contained a hole so as to expose a person to a risk to his health and safety.

(b) contrary to regulation 5(1) of the workplace (Health, Safety and Welfare) Regulations 1992 the workplace was not maintained in an efficient state, in efficient working order or in good repair.

5   The Defendant was negligent in the following respects:

(a) the above set-out breaches of statutory duty are repeated by the claimant as allegations of negligence

(b) failed to warn the claimant by means of signs, notices, marking or otherwise of the presence of a pothole in the path

(c) failed to prevent the claimant walking along the path by the use of fencing, cones, barriers or otherwise

(d) failed to inspect the path

(e) failed to repair or maintain the path

(f) failed to provide and maintain safe means of access to the claimant's place of work

(g) having a duty to carry out an assessment under regulation 3(1)(a) of the Management of Health and Safety at Work Regulations 1999, the Defendant failed to carry out a suitable and sufficient assessment of risk to the health and safety of their employees to which they were exposed whilst at work

D. Trip on retail premises

IN THE STOKESHIRE COUNTY COURT   **Case No.**   **/2003**

BETWEEN

Alf Faller	**Claimant**
and	
Acme Pie Shop Ltd	**Defendant**

PARTICULARS OF CLAIM

---

1.   At all relevant times the Defendants were the occupiers of shop premises known as "Acme Pie Shop", 1, High Street, Oldtown, Stokeshire, to which members of the public were invited for the purpose of shopping.

2.   On the   day of   2003 the Claimant lawfully entered the premises for the purpose of purchasing goods offered for sale by the Defendants. The Claimant completed his purchase and was leaving by the only door when he tripped and fell. The trip and fall was caused by a defect in the surface of the premises where the same adjoined or abutted the pavement.

3.   The Claimants accident was caused by the negligence of the defendants, their employees or agents or by breach of their statutory duty under section 2 of the Occupiers' Liability Act 1957 or both.

Details

(a) causing or permitting the defect to be or become or to remain a danger and trap to the Claimant.

(b) failing to repair the defect.

(c) failing to warn the claimant by means of signs, notices, marking or otherwise of the presence of the defect

      (d) failing to fence or guard the defect

      (e) failing to prevent the doors being used as an entrance or exit when the same led to danger and a trap, namely the defect.

      (f) in the circumstances of the case, failing to discharge their common duty of care to the Claimant in breach of the Act or otherwise.

4.   as a result of the matters detailed above the Claimant as suffered personal injury, and consequential loss.

Index

more personal injury publishing from emis professional publishing

health and safety law: a modern guide

jeffry zindani, solicitor, managing director, Forum Law

This a no-nonsense guide provides you with a comprehensive account of the law relating to health and safety.

Jeffry Zindani's book and accompanying CD enables you to check the law **quickly and easily** and apply it for your clients using practical tools such as the **Allegations Bank.**

Key contents:

- Risk Assessments and the Law
- Work Equipment
- Manual Handling
- Chemical Hazards
- Personal Protective Equipment
- Modern Health & Safety Hazards (incl Occupational Stress, RSI and Violence at Work).
- Appendices include Statutory Material, with Guidance Notes and a Case Digest and Allegations Bank for PI practitioners.

Jeffry Zindani has been described as a PI lawyer to watch (The Lawyer). He has advised claimants and trade unions with one of the country's biggest personal injury practices.

ISBN: 1 85811 217 6   New in January 2003
Paperback with updated Seneca electronic publishing version £65.00
including 2 free issues of the Seneca EP version of the newsletter below

---

Seneca CM

emis's unique and innovative Contact file and activity Management software contains a full personal injury workflow – including uncontested cases such as VWF claims.

To find out more contact us for a free video or live demonstration through www.emisit.com.

health and safety law

9 Gough Square Personal Injury and Employment Barristers

This newsletter updates the *Health and Safety Law* service, to ensure that you don't miss a key change.

Coverage in Health & Safety includes:

- Risk Assessments and the Law
- Work Equipment
- Manual Handling
- Chemical Hazards
- Personal Protective Equipment
- Modern Health & Safety Hazards (incl Occupational Stress, RSI and Violence at Work).
- Case Digest and updating articles.

9 Gough Square is one of the leading personal injury and employment sets in the country.

> A4 Newsletter and single user licence for electronic service
> Quarterly Publication: 2002   Price: £80
> 2 free electronic issues with *Health & Safety Law: A Modern Guide*

Also from emis professional publishing

---

manual handling law and litigation

For lawyers, employers and workplace safety advisers, this book will provide the ideal guide to the Manual Handling Operations Regulations 1992 and recent case law. Jeffry Zindani has handled a substantial caseload for claimants such as nurses and the police.

> £42.00   1998   ISBN 1 85811 180 3

damages

Simon Levene, Barrister, 12 Kings Bench Walk

Quantum of damages is at the heart of all Personal Injury practitioners' work. To assess quantum quickly and accurately is essential not just for the client but for the lawyer seeking to assess risk for funding.

This unique service offers:

- Speed of access
- Key information, sorted by PI practitioner's criteria

- Digests all other key sources
- Organised by injury
- Multiplier applied including automatic *Heil* v *Rankin* calculator (also usable independently on your caseload)
- Portable one volume paperback
- Updated monthly by download, ensuring you are using the latest version even on a laptop

Book and 2003 Service £149.00   Network Licence £10 + VAT per user
ISBN 1 85811 264 8
Paperback and free single user licence to electronic service

kevan on credit hire

Tim Kevan, Barrister, 1 Temple Gardens

In road traffic claims, insurance companies compensate individuals in the form of repair and/or a replacement car. A 'credit hire' and 'credit repair' industry has developed on the basis that the insurer will pay. Whether you are a claimant or defendant practitioner, this book will clearly and succinctly ensure that keep up to date with the law – including Consumer Credit issues.

£48   2002   ISBN 1 85811 275 3

children and personal injury

Andrew Hogan, Barrister, Ropewalk Chambers

This succinct and well-written book looks at the law and procedure governing the litigation of claims brought by injured children, covering the unique aspects of acting for children.

£28   2000   1 85811 262 1

medical records for lawyers

Ali Malsher BA (Hons), MA, Solicitor, Registered General Nurse

Medical areas are covered with basic anatomy and physiology, common complaints, symptoms, investigations and tests and explanation of treatments and sample medical records. You will also be able to cross-reference records to check that certain activities have been completed by the medical and nursing teams. Medical terminology, medical words and symbols are all explained succinctly.

£42   2002   ISBN 1 85811 259 1

contributory negligence

Justin Levinson, Barrister, No One Dr Johnsons Buildings

Your client's action involves mitigation because one party's contributory negligence. How can you estimate what percentage that contributory negligence should be? How can justify asking for a particular percentage in your particulars of claim or defence? Until now practitioners have not had ready access to a collection of cases, organised by type of case. Using Justin Levinson's considered and well-researched book, practitioners will now be able to quickly identify similar facts and the percentage of contributory negligence that is reasonable.

£39   2002   1 85811 292 3

work related injury litigation:
a practitioners handbook

Tim Meakin and Dr Peter Ellis, Barristers, Goldsmith Chambers

This clear and accessible book provides personal injury and clinical negligence practitioners with the only up to date single volume paperback covering this increasingly crucial area of work.

1. The legal framework
2. Deafness and tinnitus
3. Occupational cancers
4. Occupational asthma and other respiratory diseases
5. Vibration induced disorders
6. Occupational infections and skin diseases
7. Occupational upper limb and spinal disorders

Appendices

• Specimen Particulars of Claim
• Specimen Defences
• Specimen Schedules of loss and damage
• Statutes and Statutory instruments

Each chapter includes sections on practice and procedure, expert evidence and quantifying the claim.

£44   ISBN: 1 85811 315 6   April 2003

EMIS Professional Publishing, 31–33 Stonehills House, Welwyn Garden City, AL8 6PU
Tel: 01707 334823   Fax: 01707 335022   DX 144000 Welwyn Garden City
order any title online at *www.emispp.com*
contact us by email at *sales@emispp.com*